Ask Gramps

Addressing *Another* 101 Everyday
Concerns, Curiosities, and
Uncertainties of Latter-day Saints,
Young and Old

~VOLUME 2~

H. Clay Gorton

Maasai Publishing
Provo, Utah

Published by Maasai, Inc.
201 East Bay Blvd
Provo, Utah 84606

Front cover graphic design by Douglass Cole and Chad Keliiki.
Page design by www.SunriseBooks.com

2002 edition by Maasai, Inc.
Library of Congress Control Number: 2001116253
ISBN: 1-889025-06-2

Other Titles by H. Clay Gorton

LANGUAGE OF THE LORD
Horizon Publishers, August 1993
New discoveries of Chiasma in the Doctrine & Covenants

THE LEGACY OF THE BRASS PLATES OF LABAN
Horizon Publishers, November 1994
A comparison of Biblical and Book of Mormon Isaiah texts

A NEW WITNESS FOR CHRIST
Horizon Publishers, March 1997
Chiastic structures in the Book of Mormon

ASK GRAMPS, VOL 1
Maasai, Inc., 2001

ASK GRAMPS FOR TEENS
Maasai, Inc., 2002

Many of the questions asked in this second volume relate to doctrines, procedures and practices of the Church of Jesus Christ of Latter-day Saints. In attempting to provide answers to these questions, I have attempted to cite sources from the scriptures and from the published writings of the General Authorities of the Church. Nevertheless, I have no authority or commission to speak in any official way for the Church. The opinions expressed herein represent nothing more than the opinion of one of the members of the Church.

—H. Clay Gorton

www.h.clay.gorton.com

Subject Index

Foreword

The *Ask Gramps* phenomenon has swept LDS Internet circles with tens of thousands of readers, gone on to become a best-selling book, and now is poised to become a series. In his typical direct, easy-to-understand style, H. Clay Gorton–*Gramps*–fields another 101 questions from his readers in this Volume 2. That devoted readership is world-wide, thanks to the Internet. Beyond his adult audience, Gramps has also become a favorite with teens. Columns to both audiences–*Ask Gramps* and *Ask Gramps for Teens*–are regular features at www.ldsliving.com, and the best of those columns have now been gathered into three books:

Ask Gramps, Vol. I
Ask Gramps, Vol. II
Ask Gramps for Teens

The hundreds of questions and answers are catalogued in Gramps' web site: www.h.clay.gorton.com.

Enjoy this wonderful new volume. Collect them all. *Ask Gramps* provides a unique format for quick information on questions that we all have wondered about. In the words of one reader, "You are a gold mine!"

—*The Publisher*

IS IT APPROPRIATE FOR CHURCH MEMBERS TO DISPLAY A PICTURE OF THE LAST SUPPER IN THEIR HOMES?

Dear Gramps,

Last month I was baptized into the Church of Jesus Christ of Latter-day Saints. I would like to know if it is appropriate for an LDS family to display in their home a picture of The Last Supper. I notice that this is not a picture sold in the local LDS bookstore.

Barbara, from Washington

Dear Barbara,

Congratulations on your new membership in the Church of Jesus Christ of Latter-day Saints. As a new member, let me suggest something to you about the *Ask Gramps* column. We are happy to give our opinion on matters that people write in about, and we will attempt to answer your questions, but this column is nothing more or less than the opinion of one individual without any authoritative connection to the church. (In fact, it was started merely as a family project to try and answer some questions of my own grandchildren, but now has grown far beyond that initial idea). As you begin your travels in the Lord's kingdom and as you have concerns (and, by the way, it will be an exciting and eye-opening journey beyond your imagination), the place to go for these questions is to your own Bishop. He has been ordained and set apart with special gifts of discernment and is the Lord's representative to the members of his ward. He will give you authoritative answers to all your questions.

Now, my *non-authoritative* answer is: to my knowledge there are no restrictions in the church about displaying in the home any representation of the Savior or of His activities. There is no doubt in my mind that the great artists and the composers of great music were inspired by the Lord in their work and have done much to elevate and ennoble mankind. We can be lifted toward God by appreciating their great work.

—Gramps

What is the real sequence of the Creation?

Gramps,
I've read the quote by Brigham Young regarding the earth falling into our present solar system. It seems that he is saying this happened after the fall of Adam. Can you explain this and what is meant by the seven days of creation?
—dc

Dear dc,
In the same quote from Brigham Young, he says
"When the earth was framed and brought into existence and man was placed upon it, it was near the throne of our Father in heaven." (*Journal of Discourses*, Vol.17, p. 144)

Being near the throne of God, it was bathed in light. The implication of the statement by Brigham Young is not that the earth had been in darkness before it was brought into the solar system, but that when that event occurred. the sun, rather than the celestial throne of God, became the source of light for the earth.

When you refer to the scriptural reference that the earth was made in seven days, I'm sure you realize that those days were not the 24-hour periods that were defined after the earth was set up in this solar system, but rather seven periods of time of indeterminate length. The Hebrew word for day, as found in Genesis, is "yowm," which can be defined as a day of 24 hours or as an indeterminate period of time. Without a doubt the latter definition applies to the use of the word in the creation account in Genesis.
—Gramps

WERE ADAM AND EVE CREATED IN THE GARDEN OF EDEN?

Gramps,
Were Adam and Eve created in the Garden of Eden or were they created somewhere else and then placed in the garden? If they were created somewhere else, where was it?
Linda, from Utah

Dear Linda,

Adam was not created in the Garden of Eden. As a matter of fact, he helped to plant it. Brigham Young makes the following statement on the subject:

> "Though we have it in history that our father Adam was made of the dust of this earth, and that he knew nothing about his God previous to being made here, yet it is not so; and when we learn the truth we shall see and understand that he helped to make this world, and was the chief manager in that operation. He was the person who brought the animals and the seeds from other planets to this world, and brought a wife with him and stayed here. You may read and believe what you please as to what is found written in the Bible. Adam was made from the dust of an earth, but not from the dust of this earth. He was made as you and I are made, and no person was ever made upon any other principle." *(Journal of Discourses,* Vol.3, p.319)

When Adam and Eve came to the earth and were introduced by the Lord into the Garden of Eden, they and the earth were of a terrestrial glory. Therefore, it is logical to assume that they were born on a terrestrial world. When Adam fell and was expelled from the Garden, the earth became a telestial sphere.

—Gramps

WERE THE AUSTRALIAN ABORIGINES EVER EXCLUDED FROM HOLDING THE PRIESTHOOD?

Dear Gramps,

A couple of months ago in priesthood meeting, a member of our quorum stated that Australian Aborigines had been excluded from holding the priesthood until 1978, when Spencer W. Kimball declared that all worthy males could be ordained to the priesthood. (I hope you can answer this, since our resident "answer man" couldn't).

Jay

Dear Jay,

When the Australian Aborigines were first taught the gospel in 1938, there was some question as to their racial origin. The Aborigines were not actively proselyted and so only a few joined the church. However, as more were baptized, the Australian mission president wrote to the First Presidency asking for a ruling on the matter. In a letter signed by President David O. McKay and his two counselors, Hugh B. Brown and N. Eldon Tanner, dated March 11, 1964, permission was granted to ordain worthy Australian Aborigine members to the priesthood. This of course was fourteen years before the official declaration on the priesthood by President Kimball in June of 1978.

—Gramps

WHAT DOES THE CHURCH HAVE TO SAY ABOUT ABORTION?

Gramps,

I am a member but I have always wondered what the church has said about abortion.

Ashley

Dear Ashley,

The taking of a human life, either before or after birth, is a grievous sin. The fact that many people in our society promote and practice this diabolical activity in no way lessens the severity of the offense before God. President Spencer W. Kimball said,

> "Abortion is a serious sin. There is such a close relationship between the taking of a life and the taking of an embryonic child, between murder and abortion, that we would hope that mortal men would not presume to take the frightening responsibility." *(The Teachings of Spencer W. Kimball, p.188)*

We read the following specific information regarding abortion in the *Encyclopedia of Mormonism,*

> "Abortion is one of the most revolting and sinful practices of this day. Members must not submit to, be a party to, or perform an abortion. The only exceptions are when:
>
> 1. Pregnancy has resulted from incest or rape;
>
> 2. The life or health of the woman is in jeopardy, in the opinion of competent medical authority; or
>
> 3. The fetus is known, by competent medical authority, to have severe defects that will not allow the baby to survive beyond birth." *(Encyclopedia of Mormonism, Vol.3)*

The God-given gift of life is precious. To prevent its occurrence or to terminate its existence are among the most serious of sins. However, the precious nature of life is not just manifested in the coming into or going out of this world. Those two acts are but the beginning and the end. Between those two points is our daily walk. Understanding the precious nature of life, we should use the utmost care not to damage or harm it in any way. If we could feel a genuine love for our Father's other children we would extend ourselves in their behalf. The question of being kind just to those who, in our opinion, would merit our kindness would not be an issue; we would treat equally well all of our Father's children. The Savior's love and compassion were extended not only to the worthy, but to all humanity. To treat anyone in an unseemly manner in some way negates our appreciation for and understanding of the great atoning sacrifice of the Son of God.

—Gramps

DO WE ANSWER OUR OWN PRAYERS?

Dear Gramps,

I feel pretty discouraged when I pray in someone else's behalf and the prayer never seems to get answered. I was listening to a talk radio show that discussed prayer and it was mentioned that God doesn't answer prayers, we answer them ourselves in some way. Sometimes I wonder if God DOES answer prayers.

Shirley, from Colorado

Dear Shirley,

Let me ask you a few questions. Do you believe that God exists and that he is the Father of the spirits of mankind?

Furthermore we have had fathers of our flesh which corrected us, and we gave them reverence: shall we not much rather be in subjection unto the Father of spirits, and live? (Hebrews 12:9)

Do you believe that the Bible, Book of Mormon, and the Doctrine and Covenants are the word of God?

And the prayer of faith shall save the sick, and the Lord shall raise him up; and if he have committed sins, they shall be forgiven him. (James 5:15)

And the Lord provided for them that they should hunger not, neither should they thirst; yea, and he also gave them strength, that they should suffer no manner of afflictions, save it were swallowed up in the joy of Christ. Now this was according to the prayer of Alma; and this because he prayed in faith. (Alma 31:38)

And, as it is written—Whatsoever ye shall ask in faith, being united in prayer according to my command, ye shall receive. (D&C 29:6)

Do you believe that Joseph Smith was telling the truth when he said,

At length I came to the conclusion that I must either remain in darkness and confusion, or else I must do as James directs, that is, ask of God. I at length came to the determination to "ask of God," concluding that if he gave wisdom to them that lacked wisdom, and would give liberally, and not upbraid, I might venture.

So, in accordance with this, my determination to ask of God, I retired to the woods to make the attempt. It was on the morning of a beautiful, clear day, early in the spring of eighteen hundred and twenty. It was the first time in my life that I had made such an attempt, for amidst all my anxieties I had never as yet made the attempt to pray vocally. (Joseph Smith History 1:13-14)

And do you believe that in answer to that prayer he
saw two Personages, whose brightness and glory defy all description, standing above me in the air. One of them spake unto me, calling me by name and said, pointing to the other—This is My Beloved Son. Hear Him! (Joseph Smith History 1:17)

Or, do you believe in talk radio shows?
—Gramps

Is Decaf Against the Word of Wisdom?

Gramps,
We all know that the Word Of Wisdom pertains to hot drinks and has been defined as tea and coffee. We all know that tea and coffee contain caffeine and the use of either would prevent us from receiving a temple recommend. I have two questions:
1. Could the use of decaf coffee and herb tea be in violation of the Word of Wisdom?
2. If "containing caffeine" is the problem how about cola drinks? There are many other things that contain caffeine, such as chocolate and some soft drinks.
Bill, from Utah

Dear Bill,
First regarding decaf. coffee and Coke—Decaf. coffee evidently contains no caffeine and therefore shouldn't be habit forming. Coke is not formally against the Word of Wisdom since it is not mentioned in the scripture, although it is heavily loaded with caffeine. So, what's the problem? There seems to me to be a very important reason to avoid both those drinks. Each of us as members of the church has a

responsibility to represent the church in the best light possible. It is part of our responsibility as "Every member a missionary." If someone not of our faith sees us drinking either coffee or Coke—and by the way, it would be rather difficult to carry around a big sign saying, "This is only Decaf."—they could easily, and often do, make the judgement that "There goes another Mormon disobeying the tenants of his own religion!" It is highly appropriate that as members of the church, we should avoid the very appearance of evil.

Now concerning herbal tea. Herbal teas are rather common drinks and not only contain no harmful substances, but in many cases have beneficial effects on the body. Many herbs and plants have been provided by the Lord to be used for restoring health. Both the frankincense and myrrh, which were given by the Wise Men to Jesus at his birth, are oils distilled from herbs. At the time of General Moroni, about 72 B.C., the Book of Mormon account mentions the beneficial effects of plants and roots in controlling fevers:

> *And there were some who died with fevers, which at some seasons of the year were very frequent in the land—but not so much so with fevers, because of the excellent qualities of the many plants and roots which God had prepared to remove the cause of diseases, to which men were subject by the nature of the climate.* (Alma 46:40)

Also, in the Doctrine & Covenants we are counseled to use herbs for medicinal purposes:

> *And whosoever among you are sick, and have not faith to be healed, but believe, shall be nourished with all tenderness, with herbs and mild food, and that not by the hand of an enemy.* (D&C 42:43)

And the Lord states that herbs "are made for the benefit and use of man."

> *"Yea, and the herb, and the good things which come of the earth, whether for food or for raiment, or for houses, or for barns, or for orchards, or for gardens, or for vineyards; Yea, all things which come of the earth, in the season thereof, are made for the benefit and the use of man, both to please the eye and to gladden the heart."* (D&C 59:17-18)

It is well and appropriate to keep ourselves from the very appearance of evil. But, of course, partaking of the good things of the earth is not evil. Perhaps we could help others to see and rejoice in the goodness of God in providing for *"the benefit of man...both to please the eye and to gladden the heart."*

If we were to have a cup of herbal tea in a public restaurant, where it would be served in a regular tea cup, it could be assumed by others that we were drinking conventional tea. In such a case it might be prudent to avoid drinking the herbal tea to prevent the possibility of giving others a wrong impression.

Concerning all the other foods and drinks that contain caffeine, such as chocolate, it is left for each individual to use his own judgement and common sense with respect to what he takes into his body. We should use wisdom in all things. Particularly in our diet, we should avoid becoming the slave of habit or addiction to any food or drink. Obesity, for instance, often results from our inability to control our appetite and thus we impair our health. This is not against the Word of Wisdom, technically, but it is certainly against the practice of wisdom.

—Gramps

IS IT EASIER TO ACCEPT THE GOSPEL IN THE POST-MORTAL SPIRIT WORLD OR IN MORTALITY?

Dear Gramps,

Some say it is somewhat more difficult to accept the Gospel in the spirit world while another school of thought says it would be much easier inasmuch as we would have more knowledge after we pass through the veil. I was wondering which is correct.

Paul, from Kentucky

Dear Paul,

When we pass through the veil we are the same person that we were in mortality. The mind is of the spirit and the brain is the physical entity that houses the mind. At death the mind, as part of the spirit, enters the spirit world. We are the same person as we were before, with the same likes and dislikes, with the same passions and desires. However, the vices of the flesh may not be satisfied in the spirit world. The drunkard will have the same longing for drink, but no way to satisfy that longing. Will repentance be easier or more difficult? Who is to say? We know very little about that environment or how people react when they are presented with the truth. Here are some statements by General Authorities worth considering:

"So-called deathbed repentance is not part of the divine plan. It is an attempt to live after the manner of the world during the years of vigor and virility, and then to gain the rewards of the blessed without ever overcoming the lusts of the flesh, lusts that, with old age and death, cease to burn in the mortal soul. Thus Amulek continues:

Do not procrastinate the day of your repentance until the end; for after this day of life, which is given us to prepare for eternity, behold, if we do not improve our time while in this life then cometh the night of darkness wherein there can be no labor performed.

There are no redeeming doctrines, no saving ordinances, no promised kingdoms of glory for such. Those who reject the gospel in this life—having heard the word from the lips of a legal administrator and having been made aware of its glories and truths—and who then accept it in the spirit world shall go to the terrestrial kingdom." (Bruce R. McConkie, *A New Witness for the Articles of Faith,* p. 230)

"There is another question that arises here. If men can hear the Gospel in the spirit world, can they obey it fully in the spirit world? Let us look at that a little. Here are the Gospel ordinances. Are ordinances of any effect? Yes, they are. 'Except a man be born of water and of the Spirit, he cannot enter into the Kingdom of God.' Just the same as if an alien does not obey the naturalization laws he cannot become a citizen of the United States. God's house is a house of order. He has a way of His own, and he that will not accept that way cannot obtain the blessing. Then can those spirits who hear the Gospel in the spirit world obey the Gospel fully? Can they believe? Yes. Can they repent? Why not? It is the soul of man, or the spirit of man in the body, not the body, that believes. It is the spirit of man in the body that repents. What is it that obeys the ordinances? Why, the spirit. But these ordinances belong to this sphere in which we live, they belong to the earth, they belong to the flesh. Water is an earthly element composed of two gases. It belongs to this earth. What there is in the spirit world, we know little about. But here is the water in which repentant believers must be baptized. Can they be baptized in the spirit world? It appears not." (Charles W. Penrose, *Journal of Discourses, Vol.24,* p.96-p.97)

—Gramps

Did the Savior's Suffering end in Gethsemane or on the Cross?

Dear Gramps,

My understanding of the Savior's experiences during the last hours of his mortal life is that our sins were paid for by His unspeakable agony in Gethsemane and that His torturous death upon the cross was solely for the purpose of overcoming physical death—He being the "first fruits of the resurrection." However, 1 John seems to indicate that Jesus' death on the cross was also part of the needed price for mankind's redemption from sin. Please explain the purpose for these two events in the mission of Jesus.

Andrew,

Dear Andrew,

Keep in mind that the sacrifice of the Savior was an "infinite" sacrifice. The suffering of the Savior was without limit, sufficient to pay the price of all sins committed by all mortal beings everywhere, past, present, and future. His suffering in that awful experience did not end until his life was ended, from Gethsemane through Calvary. He did not say *"it is finished"* until the moment before he bowed his head and gave up the ghost.

> *"When Jesus therefore had received the vinegar, he said, It is finished: and he bowed his head, and gave up the ghost."* (John 19:30)

—Gramps

What does the term "Barak Ale" mean? It was given to Joseph Smith and recorded in the Doctrine and Covenants.

Dear Gramps,

In the early versions of the Doctrine and Covenants, Joseph Smith was referred to by the name "Barak Ale." What is the significance of

*this name? Is it in any way related to his pre-mortal identity? We know
a little bit about the pre-mortal identity and role of other prominent fig-
ures such as Gabriel. Do you have any ideas concerning the pre-mortal identity and role of Joseph Smith?*
    John Campbell

Dear John,
    Perhaps we shouldn't try to read too much into the possible signifi-
cance of the code names that were used to identify certain individuals
in earlier editions of the Doctrine and Covenants. Those code names
were used to hide the identity of various individuals because of the
threat of violence. They were later replaced by the real names after all
potential threats against the individuals had disappeared. The word
barak is a Hebrew term meaning lightning. The word *ale*, to my knowledge, has no direct equivalent in Hebrew.
    —Gramps

WHY WAS RECEIVING THE TEMPLE ENDOWMENT SUCH A STRENGTH TO THE PIONEERS?

Dear Gramps,
    *Why was the temple endowment such a strength to the pioneers as
they left Nauvoo and traveled to Salt Lake City?*
    Anonymous, from Washington

Dear Anonymous,
    The blessings made available to the children of men in God's holy
temples are the greatest blessings that are given by God to men on the
earth. The pathway to the glory of exaltation in the celestial kingdom
of God is through the doors of the temple; it can be achieved in no other
way. The Lord has said,
    *Therefore, verily I say unto you, that your anointings, and your
washings, and your baptisms for the dead, and your solemn assem-
blies...are ordained by the ordinance of my holy house, which my*

people are always commanded to build unto my holy name. (D&C 124:39)

Great strength comes to those who are endowed in the holy temples. As an example, there is a vast difference in the commitment of a person who chooses not to use tobacco, because he realizes that it is bad for his health, and a person who does not use tobacco because he has made a sacred covenant with the Lord to obey the Word of Wisdom. The choice of the first person comes from a certain rationale and judgment on his part, and he has no more obligation to follow his course than his own wisdom dictates. But to the second person, who has made a covenant of obedience with the Lord, his abstinence from the use of tobacco has become a matter of principle, and matters of principle are not open to negotiation. Thus, he who obeys a certain concept as a matter of principle has much more strength to stay his course than does a person whose judgment is a matter of convenience or rationalization. The pioneers were following the Prophet as a matter of principle; and far from being a matter of convenience, their decision to leave all their possessions and endure all the hardships and even death on their march to the West represented a great sacrifice. It was specifically their commitment to principle that gave them the strength to endure all that they had to endure to obey those who spoke for the Lord and establish the Zion of the West in fulfilment of prophecy.

—Gramps

WHY ARE WE PUNISHED BY BEING CONDEMNED TO MORTALITY BECAUSE OF THE DISOBEDIENCE OF ADAM AND EVE?

Dear Gramps,
If we are punished for our own sins and not for Adam's (or Eve's) transgression, then why is it that we must work by the sweat of our brows and in sorrow bear children?
Chip

Dear Chip,

When Adam and Eve lived in the Garden of Eden, the earth was in a terrestrial state, to which it will be returned during the Millennium. Eve, being deceived by Satan, partook of the forbidden fruit and therefore knew that she would be cast out of the Garden of Eden. Adam, rather than remaining "a lone man in the Garden," and realizing that it would be better to partake of the forbidden fruit and remain with Eve so that "man might be," knowingly partook of the fruit.

It is essential to God's plan that Adam's children work out their salvation in a telestial setting where Satan has power so that they can learn to overcome opposition and, by their own volition, choose to follow God in an environment of adversity. The opposition we experience in mortality—temptation, pain, suffering, disappointment, the necessity of physical labor to overcome an adverse environment—was not designed as a punishment but rather as a blessing. Our task is to become like the Savior. In fact, the Lord has commanded,

> *Be ye therefore perfect, even as your Father which is in heaven is perfect.* (Matthew 5:48)

In order to do so, we must overcome the world. The Lord has said,

> *For verily I say unto you, I will that ye should overcome the world; wherefore I will have compassion upon you.* (D&C 64:2)

Mortality in the telestial kingdom was not given as a punishment to man because of the acts of Adam and Eve, but as an opportunity to develop and exhibit faith in the Lord Jesus Christ, and to live by every word that proceeds forth from the mouth of God. In mortality we will be punished for our own disobedience and rewarded for our own righteousness, and to him who overcomes the greater opposition will be afforded the greater reward.

—Gramps

WHY DOES PAUL SAY THAT ADAM WAS FORMED BEFORE EVE?

Dear Gramps,

In 1 Timothy 1:13-14 it reads,

"For Adam was first formed, then Eve. And Adam was not deceived, but the woman being deceived was in the transgression."

Why does Paul say that Adam was formed before Eve? Is he simply illustrating Adam's priesthood authority, or is there more to it than that? Furthermore, what does he mean by verse 14? It seems to imply that Adam was not responsible for the Fall, but tries to blame Eve. What is the point of singling out Eve since both she and Adam were involved in the transgression? How am I to take this?

Andrew, from California

Dear Andrew,

Why is it so unusual to believe that Adam was formed before Eve? The only other alternatives are that Adam was younger or that Adam and Eve were twins.

Paul says that Adam was not deceived, meaning that it the devil tried to tempt him and Adam resisted that temptation. However, Eve WAS deceived. She succumbed to the temptation of the Adversary, partook of the forbidden fruit, and by so doing was condemned to be cast out of the Garden of Eden.

This left Adam with a problem. He had been given two commandments—to multiply and replenish the earth, and to abstain from eating the fruit of the Tree of Knowledge of Good and Evil. Eve had partaken of the fruit and would be cast out. If Adam had refused to partake of the fruit and had remained a lone man in the Garden of Eden, he would have broken the "multiply and replenish" commandment. Or, he could partake of the fruit and leave the Garden with his wife, thus making it possible for them to procreate and populate the earth. Adam was not deceived. He weighed the two alternatives and chose to transgress, if you will, the lessor of the two commandments. That is the basis for Paul's inspired remarks. You will find a rather full account of this in Moses, chapter 4.

—Gramps

How can I help a person in treatment for cancer appreciate the value of prayer?

Dear Gramps,

How can I define the value of prayer to a woman not of our faith who has been diagnosed with breast cancer and is undergoing chemotherapy and radiation? Her prognosis is not good. She asks the question, "If we lived with Heavenly Father before coming to this earth and He knows what is going to happen to us (I guess she feels that He knows she is going to die from this cancer), what's the use of others' praying for her to get better?"

Lynne, from New Zealand

Dear Lynne,

We have been commanded by the Lord to "pray always." (Luke 18:1; Luke 21:36; 2 Thessalonians 1:11; 2 Nephi 32:9; 3 Nephi 18:15,18, 19; D&C 10:5; D&C 19:38; 20:33; 31:12; 32:4; 61:39; 88:126; 90:24; 93:49; 93:50; 101:81)

If the Lord has so frequently commanded us to pray always it must surely have a deep and meaningful value; otherwise, why would we have received such a commandment? Our Heavenly Father is indeed our Father. He looks kindly on his children and is delighted to hear their petitions and delights in answering their prayers. However, He is not a parent that just grants requests so as not to be further bothered. Rather, He is a loving and kind parent, who would not accede to a request if it were not for the child's best good. He does listen to and answer the earnest prayer of faith. Perhaps the outstanding example is the appearance of an angel to the wicked son of Alma, by which he was converted to the church and became a powerfully righteous person:

> *And again, the angel said: Behold, the Lord hath heard the prayers of his people, and also the prayers of his servant, Alma, who is thy father; for he has prayed with much faith concerning thee that thou mightest be brought to the knowledge of the truth; therefore, for this purpose have I come to convince thee of the power and authority of God, that the prayers of his servants might be answered according to their faith. (Mosiah 27:14)*

One other thought—concerning terminal illness. Each of us must pass from mortality at some time or other. But that passing is not in our hands. In fact, we are almost never given to know when it may occur. Our assignment is to continue to live; to continue to struggle to live. When we leave ourselves in the Lord's hands, we do not give ourselves up to death, but to living and to life.

Our physical health is impacted by our mental attitude. This is especially so with cancer. If the person plans to recover—*really* plans to recover, the forces of the body can work together to bring that about inasmuch as it is physically possible. This body-mind relationship with respect to cancer is well developed in an interesting book by Dr. Bernie Seigel, called *Love, Medicine and Miracles*. You might consider giving it as a gift to your friend.

—Gramps

IS IT NORMAL TO BE SCARED WHEN MARRIAGE IS PENDING?

Dear Gramps,

I am wondering what some of your thoughts are on marriage. I'm 20 years old and about to make that very important decision. We've dated for over a year. Is it normal to get very scared as marriage becomes real and as I discuss it with my boyfriend? I know he is a man of God, so I don't understand why I'm so scared. I know he loves me, but how do I know if I love him? Sometimes I wonder if it's love that I feel, but I don't understand why I wouldn't love my boyfriend because he is such a good guy and completely worthy of taking me to the temple. What do these feelings mean?

Brittney, from Idaho

Dear Brittney,

You are talking about the most important decision that you will make in your entire life. (There! Does that make you feel any better?) This decision has far reaching consequences into the eternities, and it will affect generations to come. Because of that, not only is this decision one of deepest concern for you and your boyfriend, but it is of vital concern to your Father in Heaven. He has a plan for you; your life here is not just left to chance.

It is not at all uncommon in the face of such decisions to entertain some doubts as to whether to go ahead or not. But if you lack some confidence in yourself to make this decision, place your confidence in the Lord, instead. No doubt you have made this matter the subject of sincere prayer, and yet you still wonder what to do. Let's talk for a minute about two concepts—faith, and the answers to prayers.

If you have faith, which in some sense is the opposite of doubt, you will act with confidence on the knowledge that you have. As you look objectively at your situation, it appears to be very positive: "I know that he is a man of God, and I know that he loves me." Based on that knowledge and the impressions of your experience together, you can make a decision. Faith then would be to act on that decision. Once the decision is made, don't revisit it unless the relevant circumstances change.

Now concerning the answer to prayer. Some people think that prayer is answered by a burning in the bosom, as in (D&C 9:8):

> *But, behold, I say unto you, that you must study it out in your mind; then you must ask me if it be right, and if it is right I will cause that your bosom shall burn within you; therefore, you shall feel that it is right.*

That is true, but those kind of answers are generally reserved, as in Oliver's translating the Book of Mormon, for cimcustances where choices among alternatives must be made. The procedure, however, is appropriate in a general sense—*you must study it out in your mind; then you must ask me if it be right*—but the answer may come in ways much more subtle than a burning in the bosom. A much more common way in which prayers are answered is given in D&C 8:2:

> *Yea, behold, I will tell you in your mind and in your heart, by the Holy Ghost, which shall come upon you and which shall dwell in your heart.*

This means that we will think it's a good idea (the mind) and that we will feed good about it (the heart). If that is the case in your situation, accept it and get on with it. You can attribute the self doubt, nervousness, and jittery feelings to the feeble attempts of the Adversary to dissuade you from an inspired course of action. Dismiss them.

—Gramps

AREN'T ALL HOT DRINKS AGAINST THE WORD OF WISDOM?

Dear Gramps,

Concerning green tea: I have often wondered about those "non-caffeinated" teas, but always took the Word of Wisdom as it is written— no hot drinks. I have often been puzzled why we are commanded not to drink hot drinks while we serve hot chocolate at winter socials. Any thoughts as to the appropriateness of this? (For the record, I enjoy hot chocolate as much as anyone.)

Mary Catherine

Dear Mary Catherine,

Brigham Young stated that the Lord was referring to tea and coffee by the term "hot drinks." It is my opinion that the Lord was referring to content, not temperature. There is no indication anywhere that we should not take warm materials as nourishment, such as soups, broths or any food off the stove. So, please do not be concerned over the temperature of food or drink. Remember, it's a Word of WISDOM. We must be expected to use wisdom in its application.

—Gramps

WHY WOULD ADDICTIONS THAT EFFECT THE PHYSICAL BODY BE OF ANY CONCERN AFTER WE ARE DEAD?

Dear Gramps,

I've heard it said that after death the spirit has the same disposition as it did in mortality. Therefore, if weaknesses of the flesh have not been conquered previous to death, it would be so much the worse for that spirit as it attempted to overcome those weaknesses in an effort to repent and conform with Gospel principles. I have trouble with that belief because faults such as alcohol or substance abuse, or a reliance on tobacco are matters of the physical body, not the spirit. Alcohol and tobacco alter the body's cell structure, especially in the brain, thus causing the dependency, and the spirit is not made of such cells and is, therefore, not subject to such alteration and subsequent dependence. To say that a person who is a slave to alcohol in mortality will remain so in the spirit world is to say that the spirit of that person is similarly enslaved, thus debunking the teaching that the spirit and the body are separate and distinct entities. If this is true, then the inevitable conclusion one comes to is that the spirit is equally capable of mortal pollution which is difficult to understand; how can that which is purely spirit be overcome by that which is purely physical?

Richard

Dear Richard,

Your conclusion that since the body and spirit are separate the one is therefore incapable of affecting the other is a interesting assumption. You state that "the spirit is not made up of such cells and therefore could not be subject to the same afflictions and dependence." We don't know the actual composition of spirit matter or whether spirit matter has a physical equivalent at the cellular level. However, although the brain is composed of mortal, physical material, the mind, which is the spiritual function of the brain, certainly accompanies the spirit on its eternal journey. The experience of mortality, so vital to our eternal progress, is carried into the spirit world in the mind. The propensities of the mind will not change when we discard the robe of mortality. We will be the same person, think the same thoughts, have the same desires, likes and dislikes. How could we not have also the same habits?

One of the early accounts of near death experiences was recorded by George Ritchie in his book entitled, *Return From Tomorrow*. In that book he tells of being in a bar room in the presence of post-mortal spirits, who were trying to satisfy their cravings for liquor by grabbing at glasses of alcohol, but without the possibility of making contact with the glass.

One of the great purposes of mortality is to subject the body to the will of the spirit. To the extent that we are subject to bodily appetites and passions, we are subject to the temptations of the Adversary. In the spirit world Satan will claim dominion over all those spirits who have enslaved themselves by carnal desire. They will not be free from the chains of addiction that bound them in mortality.

On the other hand, those who overcome the body by the spirit and have control over themselves, and who, with that control, subject themselves to the will of the Father, will indeed be free. So I imagine that our addictions, as well as all the other propensities of the mind, will not change by merely stepping out of the body.

—Gramps

WHAT WILL HAPPEN WHEN THE SAVIOR RETURNS AT THE COUNCIL AT ADAM-ONDI-AHMAN?

Gramps,

At the time of the Savior's return to the earth, a conference is to be held at Adam-ondi-Ahman with the Savior and others. What will be the agenda of this meeting and who will be the invited guests?

Ross

Dear Ross,

The great meeting of the priesthood that was prophesied by Daniel to take place in the valley of Adam-ondi-Ahman will be one of the most momentous occasions in the history of the earth. In this great convocation the leaders of all the dispensations of the gospel will report their stewardships to Father Adam. Adam will then report to the Savior, turning his stewardship of the earth over to the Master, who, according to the established order of the Priesthood, will begin to reign on the earth as King of kings and Lord of lords.

President Joseph Fielding Smith Jr., in *The Way to Perfection*, p.290-291, described that council in the following terms:

"This council in the valley of Adam-Ondi-Ahman is to be of the greatest importance to this world. At that time there will be a transfer of authority from the usurper and impostor, Lucifer, to the rightful King, Jesus Christ. Judgment will be set and all who have held keys will make their reports and deliver their stewardships, as they shall be required. Adam will direct this judgment, and then he will make his report, as the one holding the keys for this earth, to his Superior Officer, Jesus Christ. Our Lord will then assume the reins of government; directions will be given to the Priesthood; and He, whose right it is to rule, will be installed officially by the voice of the Priesthood there assembled. This grand council of Priesthood will be composed, not only of those who are faithful who now dwell on this earth, but also of the prophets and apostles of old, who have had directing authority. Others may also be there, but if so they will be there by appointment, for this is to be an official council called to attend to the most momentous matters concerning the destiny of this earth."

We understand that this meeting will go unnoticed by the world. Even members of the who are not invited to attend may not be aware of it.

—Gramps

By what means did the Prophet Translate the Book of Mormon?

Gramps,

I would like to know the exact way the Prophet Joseph translated the Book of Mormon. For instance, I read that at first he used a seer stone instead of the Urim and Thummim, which he evidently placed in his hat, then buried his face in the hat to block out the light. If I understand it, a sentence from the plates would appear and beneath it the English translation. Do the testimonies of eye-witnesses flip-flop the seer stone with the Urim and Thummim? If not, what happened to the stone?

Al, from New York

Dear Al,

You're right, the Prophet used both the Seer Stone and the Urim and Thummim in translating the Book of Mormon. But "the exact way" in which it was done is not known. The only recorded words that the Prophet ever uttered about how he performed the translation are recorded on the title page of the Book of Mormon—*To come forth by the gift and power of God unto the interpretation thereof.*

The Seer Stone was egg-shaped and of a chocolate color. And it is true that when using the Seer Stone, at least during the daytime, the Prophet would put it in a hat and then bury his face in the hat to keep out the light, so that he could read the inscriptions that would appear on the stone. B.H. Roberts quoted David Whitmer's description of translating by the Seer Stone as follows:

> "A piece of something resembling parchment would appear, and on that appeared the writing. One character at a time would appear, and under it was the translation in English. Brother Joseph would read off the English to Oliver Cowdery, who was his principal scribe, and when it was written down and repeated to Brother Joseph to see if it were correct, then it would disappear and another character with the interpretation would appear." (B.H. Roberts, *Defense of the Faith and the Saints*, Vol.1, p.351)

The Urim and Thummim were two transparent stones arranged in a bow somewhat similar to spectacles, and were attached to a breast plate. The Prophet used either the Seer Stone or the Urim and Thummim in the translation of the Book of Mormon. B.H. Roberts comments on the use of the two instruments in the translation process as follows:

> "The sum of the whole matter, then, concerning the manner of translating the sacred record of the Nephites, according to the testimony of the only witnesses competent to testify in the matter is: With the Nephite record was deposited a curious instrument, consisting of two transparent stones, set in the rim of a bow, somewhat resembling spectacles, but larger, called by the ancient Hebrews 'Urim and Thummim,' but by the Nephites 'Interpreters.' In addition to these 'Interpreters' the Prophet Joseph had a 'Seer Stone,' possessed of similar qualities to the Urim and Thummim; that the prophet sometimes used one and sometimes the other of these sacred instruments in the work of translation; that whether the 'Interpreters' or the 'Seer Stone' was used the Nephite characters with the English

interpretation appeared in the sacred instrument; that the Prophet would pronounce the English translation to his scribe, which when correctly written would disappear and the other characters with their interpretation take their place, and so on until the work was completed." (B.H. Roberts, *The Seventy's Course in Theology, First Year*, p.111)

—Gramps

WHERE CAN I FIND AN ACCOUNT OF THE FOUNDING FATHERS' COMING TO THE ST. GEORGE TEMPLE?

Gramps,
I am looking for an account of the Founding Fathers' coming to the St. George Temple to have their temple work done. There is a painting of this event in the Washington, D.C. Temple. Where can I find this account?
Steve, from Utah

Dear Steve,
There are numerous references to the ordinance work that was done for the Founding Fathers in the St. George Temple in 1877. President Ezra Taft Benson spoke a number of times of the event. Here is an excerpt of one of his statements printed in the *Church News*, Feb. 28, 1989.

"Shortly after President Spencer W. Kimball became president of the church, he assigned me to go into the vault of the St. George Temple and check the early records. As I did so, I realized the fulfillment of a dream I had had ever since learning of the visit of the Founding Fathers to the St. George Temple. I saw with my own eyes the record of the work which was done for the Founding Fathers of this great nation, beginning with George Washington.

"Think of it, the Founding Fathers of this nation, those great men, appeared within those sacred walls and had their vicarious work done for them.

"After he became president of the church, President Wilford Woodruff declared that 'those men who laid the foundation of this American government were the best spirits the God of heaven could find on the face of the earth. They were choice spirits...and were inspired of the Lord." (*Church News*, Feb. 28, 1989.)

On the occasion of the 500th anniversary of the voyage of Columbus to the New World, President Benson made the following declaration concerning Christopher Columbus and the other 'eminent men' whose temple ordinances were performed by President Woodruff:

"The temple work for the fifty-six signers of the Declaration of Independence and other founding fathers has been done. All these appeared to Wilford Woodruff when he was President of the St. George Temple. President George Washington was ordained a High Priest at that time. You will also be interested to know that according to Wilford Woodruff's journal, John Wesley, Benjamin Franklin, and Christopher Columbus were also ordained High Priests at the time. When one casts doubt upon the character of these noble sons of God, I believe he or she will have to answer to the God of heaven for it." (Arnold K. Garr, *Epilogue, Christopher Columbus*, p.72)

—Gramps

How can I influence my Agnostic friend for the better?

Dear Gramps,

I have just recently found out that my friend has absolutely no belief in God. She believes in the theory of evolution. I believe in God and our Savior Jesus Christ. She cannot believe in a God who would allow horrific, long suffering and death to happen to innocent little children. She believes that man made up the story of God to explain "human existence." She doesn't believe that the Bible is anything but a storybook. How does one touch such an individual? I've shared my testimony and my beliefs. How can one reach someone that believes that we are merely born, live, and die? Thanks.

June, from California

Dear June,

Your friend is like many others who try to explain religion intellectually rather than spiritually. Attempting to apply man's reasoning to God's work is a futile exercise and leads to many errors. Although it is not difficult to explain the logic of God's work, all logical arguments are based on certain *a priori* premises. If one does not accept the *a priori* premises, there is no basis for logical communication. In addition, true conversion to the principles of truth has never followed the path of intellectual reasoning.

The ways of God are so far beyond the ways of man that there is only one way that any knowledge of God or of His works may be obtained, and is by direct revelation. His revelations are recorded in the Holy Scriptures and in the words of modern-day Prophets. In addition, each individual, if he qualifies, may also receive direct revelation from God confirming the words of the prophets and the scriptures.

Testimony, not logic, converts. When testimony is borne, the Holy Spirit carries the words to the hearts of the listeners to the extent that they are prepared to be influenced by the Holy Spirit.

You have done a good thing by bearing your testimony to your friend. The other thing that you could do would be to so live your religion that your friend will want to share the joy that you receive from obeying the commandments. Then she may develop a willing heart.

It is counter-productive to contend with her about the principles of the gospel. Contention is of the Adversary and promotes ill will rather than learning. Let your friend know that you respect her beliefs and that you are a true friend. She must find her own way.

—Gramps

WHAT HAPPENED TO THE ARK OF THE COVENANT?

Gramps,

Do we know what happened to the Ark of the Covenant? I have heard a few different opinions and I was just wondering.

—Confused in California

Dear Confused,

The Ark of the Covenant was constructed while the children of Israel were wandering in the desert after their escape from the Egyptians. It held the things that were sacred to people at the time, including the two tablets of stone that Moses brought down from the mountain. The tribe of Levi was commissioned to the care of the ark. After the construction of Solomon's Temple, it was placed there, in the Holy of Holies. Later it was captured by the Philistines, who held it for seven months before it was returned to the Israelites. The House of Judah was taken captive by Nebuchadnezzar and carried way into Babylon in 589 B.C. They were permitted to return to Jerusalem in 519 B.C., when they immediately set about to build another temple, which was called the Temple of Zerubbabel.

We learn from James E. Talmage, that in the Temple of Zerubbabel the Most Holy Place was empty, "for the Ark of the Covenant had not been known after the people had gone into captivity." (*The House of the Lord*, p.42) So, we can only imagine that the Ark of the Covenant was taken by the Babylonians at the capture of Jerusalem, and has never been heard from since.

—Gramps

WHY DOES THE CONGREGATION SAY 'AMEN' AFTER A PRAYER OR A TALK?

Gramps,

Do we always have to say 'amen' after the person praying has said Amen? And after a talk is given and the speaker says 'amen,' is there some requirement that we repeat 'amen,' or is it just a custom? If so, why?

Eva

Dear Eva,

The repeating of "amen" by the congregation after a prayer or a discourse is a very old custom dating from biblical times. The Hebrew word, "amen" was adopted into the Greek language, then into Latin, and then in English by the 12ᵗʰ century. The word, "amen" in Hebrew means "so be it." It has the same meaning in Greek when used at the end of a prayer or discourse. However, in Greek it may be used at the beginning of a discourse, to mean "surely, truly, of a truth."

The repeating of the word by members of the congregation is their affirmation of what was said—a verbal expression of concurrence or agreement. So it is customary and appropriate in our church meetings to voice approval of the prayer or discourse by repeating the word "amen."

The practice varies from congregation to congregation. In some wards, one hears an enthusiastic response by the congregation. In others, no verbal expression is heard. This indicates that the practice is somewhat habitual, and that members tend to follow along with the established practice. However, it would seem appropriate for us to listen carefully to the prayers that are offered and the talks that are given so that at the end we could voice our support, approval, and concurrence with what was spoken and our commitment to comply with the counsel given.

—Gramps

WHERE AND HOW OFTEN SHOULD MISSIONARIES BE FED?

Dear Gramps,
Can you please tell me where it is outlined about members' feeding the missionaries and how often they should be fed? Thank you.
skm, from Michigan

Dear skm,
I don't think that you will find a church directive on the care and feeding of missionaries. They normally should be fed three times a day. However, they would eat more often if you would let them. When left

on their own, both the quality and the quantity of their dietary intake may suffer. Quantity goes up and quality goes down.

Their eating habits vary according to the mission to which they are called and according to the Ward or Branch in which they are serving. In some units, the local members are so organized that the missionaries never have to ask for a meal. They just follow the printed schedule. In other areas, they graciously make appointments to visit the member just at meal time (when everyone will be home) and sometimes they are invited to stay for dinner.

Members should be sensitive to the culinary likes and dislikes of missionaries, especially those who are serving in countries other than their country of origin. It is often difficult for young people to quickly adapt to a dietary regime with which they are not familiar.

Members should also be careful not to be overly friendly or familiar with the missionaries. Their activities and their time are rather restricted. I understand that they shouldn't spend more than an hour in a member's home at mealtime.

In some areas, missionaries are supposed to board with people who are not members of the church. This gives them an opportunity to share the spirit of the gospel and hopefully find teaching opportunities with their hosts. If you ever see a missionary sitting listlessly on a street corner he usually can be revived by a candy bar or a milk shake.

—Gramps

IS THE CONCEPT OF
BLOOD ATONEMENT TRUE?

Dear Gramps,

I would like to point out that there is a lot of stuff, pro and con, about the church, which we may or may not like. The Lord's gospel is true, but His people aren't sometimes. I only want to know, is the concept of blood atonement true?

amj, from Holland

Dear amj,

It never ceases to amaze me how some members of the church, who should know better, seem to continually turn to fables, an obvious fulfilment of Paul's prophecy recorded in 2 Timothy 4:3-4:

> *For the time will come when they will not endure sound doctrine; but after their own lusts shall they heap to themselves teachers, having itching ears; And they shall turn away their ears from the truth, and shall be turned unto fables.*

They seem to put more credence in what the protestors have to say than in the words of the Prophets. I don't understand why there is such a desire to examine and investigate every protestation of evil against the church. We always tend to find what we look for whether it is there or not.

Such ruminations should be beneath the dignity of those who profess to have testimonies of the gospel. Rather than looking for every bad thing that is professed by the detractors, why not bend one's energies to looking for every good thing that the Lord's kingdom has to offer?

Nevertheless, here is the specific answer to your question on blood atonement—if you can accept the words of the prophets over those of evil men who are trying to tear down the Kingdom of God.

"From the days of Joseph Smith to the present, wicked and evilly-disposed persons have fabricated false and slanderous stories to the effect that the church, in the early days of this dispensation, engaged in a practice of blood atonement whereunder the blood of apostates and others was shed by the church as an atonement for their sins. These claims are false and were known by their originators to be false. There is not one historical instance of so-called blood atonement in this dispensation, nor has there been one event or occurrence whatever, of any nature, from which the slightest inference arises that any such practice either existed or was taught." (Bruce R. McConkie, *Mormon Doctrine*, p.92)

—Gramps

WHEN DID DINOSAURS LIVE ON THE EARTH?

Gramps,
After visiting the dinosaur museum in Vernal, Utah recently, I again pondered the question, "When did the dinosaurs live upon the earth?" Was it before the Garden of Eden period, or when? Could you enlighten me on this subject? Thank you!
Anonymous, from Utah

Dear Anonymous,

No time scale for events prior to the Garden of Eden experience are given in the scriptures. There are some things, however, that we can piece together concerning this period. When the earth was created, it was a terrestrial sphere and did not become a telestial world until Adam and Eve partook of the forbidden fruit. No time line is given either for the interval between their partaking of the fruit and their expulsion from the garden. Indications are that they were expelled from the garden near the beginning of the first thousand years of the earth's temporal existence, *i.e.* ~4000 B.C.

Prehistoric time measurement is questionable. One of the reasons for this is that all scientific conclusions are based on certain assumptions that are *not* called into question. These "givens" form the present scientific foundation for the structure of the logic upon which the conclusions are based. They are called *a priori* assumptions.

Let's examine a few assumptions upon which scientific time lines are based. A principle assumption is that the earth has had a benign history. That is, that the processes that effect the earth's topology, which are prominent in today's scientific thinking—wind, rain, freezing and thawing, the imperceptibly slow drift of the tectonic plates and continental uplift—have *always* been the major influences that have caused the earth to change and have *always* occurred at the same rate that they do today. This theory is called "uniformitarianism."

An opposing theory suggests that the earth has had a cataclysmic history, *i.e.*, that the surface of the earth has been abruptly changed by great cataclysmic events, such as major volcanoes, earthquakes, floods, and impacts by space debris.

Up until the time of Sir Isaac Newton, the cataclysmic theory held sway, and Newton was one of its proponents. But, following an epic debate on the subject, the uniformitarianism theory won the day and has been accepted by the scientific world ever since. However, there is some scriptural information and writings by the Brethren, in addition to a preponderance of recently discovered information about the history of the earth, that strongly supports the cataclysmic theory.

Here are just two of the cataclysmic events mentioned in the scriptures: 1) the universal flood; and 2) the division of the earth in the days of Peleg.

From the writings of the prophets there is more information. For example, in 1874, Brigham Young made this very interesting statement about the history of the earth:

"This earth is our home, it was framed expressly for the habitation of those who are faithful to God, and who prove themselves worthy to inherit the earth when the Lord shall have sanctified, purified and glorified it and brought it back into his presence, from which it fell far into space.... When the earth was framed and brought into existence and man was placed upon it, it was near the throne of our Father in heaven. And when man fell...the earth fell into space, and took up its abode in this planetary system, and the sun became our light. When the Lord said— 'Let there be light,' there was light, for the earth was brought near the sun that it might reflect upon it so as to give us light by day, and the moon to give us light by night. This is the glory the earth came from, and when it is glorified it will return again unto the presence of the Father, and it will dwell there, and these intelligent beings that I am looking at, if they live worthy of it, will dwell upon this earth." (*Journal of Discourses*, Vol.17, p.144)

We understand from Brigham Young that before the fall of man the earth was located near the celestial throne of God, and that it is a relative newcomer to the our solar system. Since the scientific community cannot interface with such a condition, as no physical evidence for it seems to exist, it cannot be a part of their rationale. However, the prophets have spoken and we know that their words are the words of God. So, since the scientific community does not necessarily have all or any of the answers regarding the physical condition of the earth prior to the Fall, science's time estimates for conditions prior to 4000 B.C. must be held in question. We will have no definite information on the history of the earth and the life that was placed upon it prior to the advent of mortal man until that information is revealed to us by the Lord.

—Gramps

CAN A WOMAN CAST OUT SATAN?

Gramps,

Is it wrong for a woman to cast out Satan if her priesthood holder husband is present but not understanding the need at the time?

What words should be used when casting out dark spirits? And how can one know if it is needed or appropriate? When our home becomes contentious or a family member is very much out of sorts, I have found that simply asking God that the evil spirits and contention be removed from our home has made an evident difference. But I do not want to offend the Lord by the overuse of this request, and I would never wish to overstep my husband's priesthood. Thanks.

Lyn, from Idaho

Dear Lyn,

One cannot invoke the power of the priesthood if one does not hold the priesthood. However, the prayer of faith availeth much. But, a prayer is a request, not a command. If we, in righteousness, plead with the Father for His blessings, He will surely hear us. Remember, prayers are answered in His way, not necessarily our way. If we know we are worthy, we will know that the Lord will hear our prayers, and we will know that He will answer them in His own way for our benefit, blessing and happiness. Thus, we are in a position to accept whatever may come and move ahead with confidence. We have been told to:

Search diligently, pray always, and be believing, and all things shall work together for your good, if ye walk uprightly and remember the covenant wherewith ye have covenanted one with another. (D&C 90:24)

Therefore, he giveth this promise unto you, with an immutable covenant that they shall be fulfilled; and all things wherewith you have been afflicted shall work together for your good, and to my name's glory, saith the Lord. (D&C 98:3)

—Gramps

Is Depression a Medical Condition or just a Bad Attitude?

Dear Gramps,

I suffered from depression after my first child and was put on Zoloft. Things got better and after a year or so, I got off the medication. Now, (after my 3rd child) I'm diagnosed with dithsemnia— depression. I'm on Zoloft again. My question is how the church feels about medication for depression. Depression seems to run in my family; however, sometimes I wonder if it's hereditary or just a bad attitude that I should fix. I don't know what's right. Worse...since I've been on this medication for depression, I no longer feel sad all the time, or think about death all the time, or hate everyone and myself...but I don't feel anything! I don't feel nervous or scared when I give a talk in church, or when we have a very trying challenge in our family, I logically think...oh that's terrible...but I don't feel that way...almost like my emotions are numbed. Can this be right? I don't feel like I can feel the spirit either. I "know" logically that the church is true...but I'm having a hard time "feeling" it. HELP!!

Ellie

Dear Ellie,

Think about a person who had just broken his arm, and before having it set, attended Sacrament meeting in great pain. He would probably have a difficult time concentrating on what was being said from the pulpit and feeling the spirit of the meeting. I doubt, however, that he should question his testimony just because, due to his physical circumstance, he didn't have the euphoric feelings that one sometimes experiences in an inspiring situation.

But you might say that his pain was in his arm. But actually, the pain was in his head. Although the nervous system directs our attention to the point of injury, if one were to cut the nerve path to the brain, the pain would not be felt. So I don't see how your feelings of depression are different from his feelings of pain.

I don't think he would feel guilty because his broken arm hurt. Nor should a depressed person feel guilty because of the depression. I'm sure that the church would not object to taking medication for depression any more than it would object to having a doctor set a broken arm.

If you know logically that the church is true, then you know it! Although testimony sometimes stems from spiritual experiences that may be associated with a high emotional factor, the truths that comprise the testimony must be independent of emotion. I hope that you can feel comfortable and secure in your knowledge of the truth, and not let it depend on the state of your health.

—Gramps

How can I help my Inactive Daughter?

Gramps,
My daughter married a man of another religion seven years ago. Both her father and I have raised her in the Mormon faith. She will not attend our church, and her husband doesn't attend his church either. What's a mother to do?
Barbara, from California

Dear Barbara,

As the parents of your daughter, you and your husband undoubtedly have already done all that a mother and father should do. We each have our free agency and are responsible for our own choices. So many times when a child goes astray, the parent will say, "It's all my fault. Where did I go wrong?" To such parents I ask a simple question, "When you were younger did you ever do anything that your parents didn't approve of?" The answer always is, "Oh yes, several things." The next question, "And do you blame your parents for what you did?" And the answer again always is, "Certainly not. It was my own decision, against the advice of my parents." So, if your parents are not to be blamed for your actions, neither are you to be blamed for the actions of your adult children, if you have done what you can to teach them what is right.

But there are some very positive things that a mother can do in situations like yours.

1) It is extremely important that your daughter feels in her heart that you love her in spite of her decision to adopt a life style different from what she was taught. Can you imagine her feelings of guilt and/or resentment if she felt that you condemned her for her actions? She must think a great deal of the person she married to give up her faith for him; and her decision must have been very difficult for her to made. Could you help her to feel that although you don't agree with her decision (She already knows that!) you admire her courage for standing up for what she thought was the appropriate thing to do, and that you love her and that you accept her decision and will support her in it?

2) Those who are brought up in the church always have something tugging at their conscience that beckons them back home. We all seem to think that the moment of today is cast in concrete and that as it is today so it will always be. But this is never the case. Life is as fluid as a stream. One's path may change by circumstances that are completely unforeseen. Our Heavenly Father has not lost sight of his daughter. He loves her and longs for her return even more than you do. I would suggest that you might direct your efforts to establishing and maintaining the best possible relationship with your daughter and her family and leave her return to the Kingdom in the hands of her Father in Heaven. Keep in mind, you can do nothing better for your daughter than pour your heart out to God both morning and night, pleading for His intervention, so that she will be guided back to the Kingdom and bring her family with her.

—Gramps

DOES "WHEAT FOR MAN" MEAN THAT WE SHOULD NOT EAT OTHER GRAINS?

Dear Gramps,
In D&C 89:17, where it says,

"Nevertheless, wheat for man, and corn for the ox, and oats for the horse, and rye for the fowls and for swine and for all beasts of the field, and barley for all useful animals, and for mild drinks, as also other grain," what exactly does this mean? It seems to me that we're told that wheat to eat and barley for mild drinks are best for us, "all grains are good for the food of man...nevertheless wheat for man, and corn for the ox..." etc. Are these other grains mentioned not good for us? Also rice and millet are just a few grains that aren't mentioned at all, and it seems to me that these would be part of "all grains" that are good for man because we don't see an "exception" made for them. Am I way off? I've always wanted to know what was meant by all of this.

Katie,

Dear Katie,

I wouldn't suggest that the other grains that are mentioned in the Word of Wisdom are not good for us because in verse 14 we are told that *all grain is ordained for the use of man and of beasts*, and in verse 16 that *all grain is good for the food of man.*

Brigham Young, in 1863, told the people,

"Sixteen years ago, when we were camped upon this temple block, I told the people that there existed, in the elements around us in these mountain regions, wheat, corn, rye, oats, barley, flax, hemp, silk and every element for producing the necessary articles used by man for food, raiment and shelter." (*Journal of Discourses,* Vol.10, p.201)

I am not a nutritionist, but I would imagine that different grains are most appropriately suited for different animals, and that all have nutritional value for all animals. I do know that the revelation came from the Lord and that He is not capricious. The Lord has his reasons for the preference, but He indicates than none of the grains should be excluded from the diets of either man or animals. Perhaps some nutritionist who reads this column could shed more light on the subject.

—Gramps

WHERE DOES THE SPIRIT GO AFTER IT LEAVES THE BODY?

Dear Gramps:

I recently attended the funeral of relatives of mine, a couple who died from the tragic circumstances of murder and suicide. I attended with sympathy and compassion in my heart. When I arrived at the viewing, I felt their distinct "spirits" lingering. I have never experienced that before. I felt the personality of the wife present, that she was extremely angry over the circumstances of her death. I did not feel the husband's presence as strongly. Yet his spirit was there, and I felt a feeling of evil that surprised me. My husband said he had exactly the same feelings.

Are we imagining this? I always thought that when the spirit left the body it immediately went to the Spirit World and did not return to this realm until the resurrection. What were we experiencing?

Brenda

Dear Brenda,

The spirit world is on this earth and in our surroundings. If we could see into the spirit world we would see that we are not alone. President Brigham Young has said:

"It reads that the spirit goes to God who gave it. Let me render this scripture a little plainer; when the spirits leave their bodies they are in the presence of our Father and God, they are prepared then to see, hear and understand spiritual things. But where is the spirit world? It is incorporated within this celestial system. Can you see it with your natural eyes? No. Can you see spirits in this room? No. Suppose the Lord should touch your eyes that you might see, could you then see the spirits? Yes, as plainly as you now see bodies, as did the servant of Elijah. If the Lord would permit it, and it was his will that it should be done you could see the spirits that have departed from this world, as plainly as you now see bodies with your natural eyes." (*Discourses of Brigham Young*, p.376 - p.377)

—Gramps

DID THE SAVIOR'S ATONEMENT PAY FOR THE SIN OF MURDER?

Dear Gramps,

I read recently that the crucifixion of Christ didn't atone for all sins. Some sins, such as murder, require a blood sacrifice and this is the idea behind capital punishment. I find this all very confusing. Could you possibly shed some light on the issue?

—ac

Dear ac,

There is NO sin for which the sacrifice of Christ did not atone. He paid the price through his unspeakable suffering for every sin that ever was or ever will be committed by every living being. There are no exceptions! His sacrifice was infinite in its scope. Being infinite, it was without bounds, without limits. The infinite nature of the great atoning sacrifice of the redeemer of mankind is revealed by Alma in the Book of Mormon:

> *For it is expedient that an atonement should be made; for according to the great plan of the Eternal God there must be an atonement made, or else all mankind must unavoidably perish; yea, all are hardened; yea, all are fallen and are lost, and must perish except it be through the atonement which it is expedient should be made. For it is expedient that there should be a great and last sacrifice; yea, not a sacrifice of man, neither of beast, neither of any manner of fowl; for it shall not be a human sacrifice; but it must be an infinite and eternal sacrifice.* (Alma 34:9-10)

> *And behold, this is the whole meaning of the law, every whit pointing to that great and last sacrifice; and that great and last sacrifice will be the Son of God, yea, infinite and eternal.* (Alma 34:14)

It is amazing how lying, false priests have distorted the truths of the gospel of Jesus Christ as it was revealed to the prophet, Joseph Smith. The great sacrifice of the Savior was the blood sacrifice. *The blood of Jesus Christ his Son cleanseth us from all sin.* (1 John 1:7) His suffering was so intense that it caused him to bleed at every pore

> *For behold, I, God, have suffered these things for all, that they might not suffer if they would repent; But if they would not repent they*

must suffer even as I; Which suffering caused myself, even God, the greatest of all, to tremble because of pain, and to bleed at every pore, and to suffer both body and spirit. (D&C 19:16-18)

Evil and conspiring men in the early days of the church distorted this pure doctrine, and with blasphemy accused the Lord's church of requiring the blood of the sinner to pay for his own sins. This blasphemous concept negates the infinite nature of the great sacrifice of the Savior, and is patently false, and never was nor could have been entertained by the church that bears His name. Elder Bruce R. McConkie had the following to say on the subject:

"From the days of Joseph Smith to the present, wicked and evilly-disposed persons have fabricated false and slanderous stories to the effect that the church, in the early days of this dispensation, engaged in a practice of blood atonement whereunder the blood of apostates and others was shed by the church as an atonement for their sins. These claims are false and were known by their origina tors to be false. There is not one historical instance of so-called blood atonement in this dispensation, nor has there been one event or occurrence whatever, of any nature, from which the slightest inference arises that any such practice either existed or was taught." (Bruce R. McConkie, *Mormon Doctrine,* p. 92)

However, the Savior's sacrifice consists of a conditional and an unconditional part. The unconditional part is the universal resurrection, by which every living thing that has experienced mortality, being born, living and dying, including all plant and all animal life, will live again in an immortal state. The conditional part has to do with the forgiveness of sin. All sin may be forgiven except the sin against the Holy Ghost, but the only sins that will be forgiven will have been committed by those who will have thoroughly repented from them and who will have relied on the merits of the Savior as the author and the finisher of their salvation.

—Gramps

In a letter from Joseph Smith to his wife, to what did the terms "Old Major" and "Little Prattlers" refer?

Gramps,
A church friend gave me a copy of a letter written by the Prophet Joseph to his wife Emma while in Liberty Jail. (dated March 21, 1839) Could you please interpret the beginning of the fourth paragraph for me? It reads:
"I want you to try to gain time and write me a long letter and tell me all you can and even if OLD MAJOR is alive yet and what those LITTLE PRATTLERS say that cling around your neck."
Jeffrey, from Alabama

Dear Jeffrey,
"Old Major" was the name of the Prophet's dog. The word "prattler" was a term in common use in Joseph's time for little children. The noun comes from the verb, "to prattle," which means "to speak in an unaffected or childish manner." The word comes from the low German, pratelen. It's first recorded use was in 1532.
—Gramps

What were the ordinances performed in the Kirtland and Nauvoo temples?

Gramps,
What ordinances were performed in the Kirtland Temple and what ordinances were performed in the Nauvoo Temple? Thanks.
Beth, from Maryland

Dear Beth,
We read from President Joseph Fielding Smith that the purpose of the Kirtland Temple was not for performing the saving ordinances but

"to provide a sanctuary where the Lord could send messengers from his presence to restore priesthood and keys held in former dispensations, so that the work of gathering together all things in one in the dispensation of the fulness of times might go on." (Joseph Fielding Smith Jr., *Doctrines of Salvation*, Vol.2, p.236)

However, some endowment work was done in the Kirtland Temple. The Prophet Joseph Smith recorded the following:
"On the twenty-first day of January, 1836, the First Presidency, and a number of the presiding brethren in the church, assembled in the Kirtland Temple where they engaged in the ordinances of the endowment, as far as it had at that time been revealed." (*Teachings of the Prophet Joseph Smith*, Section Two 1834–37, p.106)

Concerning the Nauvoo Temple, we also learn from President Joseph Fielding Smith that—
"When the Nauvoo Temple was built, it was perfected in all details according to the vision given to the Prophet Joseph Smith. This is also true of all the temples constructed since that time in the Church." (Joseph Fielding Smith Jr., *Doctrines of Salvation*, Vol.2, p.236)

Baptisms, endowments and sealings were performed in the Nauvoo Temple, but no vicarious work was carried out there. We learn again from Joseph Fielding Smith, (*Doctrines of Salvation*, Vol.2, p.171) that the first vicarious work was carried out in the St. George Temple, the first temple to be completed after the Saints had settled in the West.
—Gramps

HOW WILL THOSE WHO LIVE DURING THE MILLENNIUM BE TESTED IF SATAN IS BOUND?

Dear Gramps,
Since one of the purposes of our coming to earth is to be tested to see whether we will choose right or wrong, how will those who live during the millennium be tested when Satan is bound?
Kristen, from California

Dear Kristen,

Those born during the Millennium will live in a blessed state, free from the temptations of Satan. However, each person will retain his or her free agency and may choose right or wrong. Even without the temptings of Satan, a person may decide to do that which is contrary to the will of our Father in Heaven. As a matter of fact, near the end of the thousand years, men will again begin to deny that there is a God. At that time, Satan will be released and will be permitted to tempt those who have been born during the Millennium, and then the end will come. Some related scriptures are listed below:

> And when the thousand years are expired, Satan shall be loosed out of his prison. (Revelation 20:7)

> And again, verily, verily, I say unto you that when the thousand years are ended, and men again begin to deny their God, then will I spare the earth but for a little season. (D&C 29:22)

> For Satan shall be bound, and when he is loosed again he shall only reign for a little season, and then cometh the end of the earth. (D&C 43:31)

Of course, we remember other blessed times, approaching that which will be experienced during the Millennium, when, through the righteousness of the people, Satan was effectively bound—Enoch's city, Melchizedek's city, the Nephites after the coming of Christ. Those people still had a mortal experience and had to choose to live the way they did.

—Gramps

WHY WAS DAVID, WHO HAD BEEN ANOINTED TO REPLACE SAUL AS KING, SO LOYAL TO HIM?

Dear Gramps,

Saul was the Lord's anointed and he became unrighteous. Samuel then anointed David. Why did David remain so loyal to Saul and honor him even though David had been anointed to be the new king and Saul was trying to kill him?

Mindi, from Michigan

Dear Mindi,

Samuel anointed David to be the eventual king of Israel and that was before David had any contact with Saul. We read from the scripture that when David was anointed by Samuel *the Spirit of the Lord came upon him from that day forward*, but it departed from King Saul. To soothe Saul's troubled mind, his servants suggested that David, who was an accomplished harpist, be called to come to Saul's court to play the harp for him. We are told that David loved Saul greatly and became his armor bearer. Shortly, however, through jealousy and fear, Saul became David avowed enemy.

From the first moment of David's association with Saul, the king knew that David would replace him. As you know, David had many opportunities to take Saul's life, yet, he was loyal to the throne. Rather than honoring Saul, it seems that David honored the office of king of the people for which Saul had been anointed by a servant of the Lord.

David provided a worthy example for all of us to follow in our ecclesiastical relationships. First, we know that there are no perfect people. Even those anointed by the Lord to preside over us in our day, our bishops and stake presidents, are not immune from iniquity and error. There are among us those who would like to take matters into their own hands and depose one in authority because of their impression of a leader's wrong doing. Such feelings and actions are never appropriate. The Lord is in control of His kingdom. Saul suffered the consequences of his own iniquity and the Lord removed him from office in His own way and in His own time. How appropriate it is for us to follow David's example and to love and sustain those who preside over us as long as they remain in the office of their callings.

—Gramps

ARE INTERRACIAL MARRIAGES ACCEPTABLE?

Gramps,
Could you please tell me the church's view of interracial marriages?
Anonymous, from Idaho

Dear Anonymous,

I can't quote you the church's official view on interracial marriage, but the following comment made by President Spencer W. Kimball to Indian students at Brigham Young University on 5 January 1965 may be enlightening.

> "Now, the brethren feel that it is not the wisest thing to cross racial lines in dating and marrying. There is no condemnation. We have had some of our fine young people who have crossed the lines. We hope they will be very happy, but experience of the brethren through a hundred years has proved to us that marriage is a very difficult thing under any circumstances and the difficulty increases in inter-race marriages."

—Gramps

WHY DON'T MISSIONARIES GIVE A MORE DETAILED EXPLANATION OF THE DOCTRINE OF SALVATION?

Gramps,

I have been going to the discussions of a woman whom my husband and I met at church. The missionaries introduced her to us because she is Catholic and my husband was Catholic before he joined the church. She is golden and accepts all that she hears. I am not happy with the way the missionaries have answered her questions about salvation. In LDS doctrine, there are three different kinds of salvation. In your opinion how would you describe salvation? She is very bright, and I know she would understand something more involved.

Donna

Dear Donna,

I wouldn't worry too much about what the missionaries are telling their investigator. It's not the doctrine that is preached that converts the investigator, but the witness of the Holy Spirit that comes to a person when the missionaries testify to the truthfulness of the gospel.

Actually, all but the sons of Perdition are saved in one kingdom or another. But to dig that deeply during the missionary discussions usually adds confusion and may detract from the Spirit. There is lots of learning time after baptism. If you add your testimony to that of the missionaries, it will have a powerful effect on the investigator, as the investigator sees you as a lay member and not a member of the clergy.

—Gramps

HAS ANYONE SEEN JOHN THE BELOVED SINCE BIBLICAL TIMES?

Dear Gramps,

When I was a Catholic school teacher, we were told to teach our students that there has been no new revelation since the last apostle died. Now that I belong to the Church of Jesus Christ of Latter-day Saints, I have learned that the last apostle is still alive, which certainly puts a new perspective on revelation from the Catholic point of view. My question is, has anyone seen John? Has his presence been detected anywhere in the past two millennia? Thanks,

Colleen, from New Mexico

Dear Colleen,

Yes, John continues his work and has been seen by many. We have specific records of only a few of those to whom John has appeared, but as you will see below, he has a great mission and is very active among those to who whom he administers. And more is yet to come.

In the first place, John appeared with Peter and James to ordain Joseph Smith and Oliver Cowdery to the Melchizedek Priesthood:

> *And again, what do we hear? Glad tidings from Cumorah! Moroni, an angel from heaven, declaring the fulfilment of the prophets—the book to be revealed. A voice of the Lord in the wilderness of Fayette, Seneca county, declaring the three witnesses to bear record of the book! The voice of Michael on the banks of the Susquehanna, detecting the devil when he appeared as an angel of light! The voice of Peter, James, and John in the wilderness between Harmony, Susquehanna county, and Colesville, Broome county, on*

the Susquehanna river, declaring themselves as possessing the keys of the kingdom, and of the dispensation of the fulness of times! (D&C 128:20, also see Joseph Smith History 1:72)

At the dedication of the Kirtland Temple, the Savior, Moses, Elias and Elijah appeared to Joseph Smith and Oliver Cowdery and committed to them the keys of their dispensations. Elias committed to the Prophet *the dispensation of the gospel of Abraham, saying that in us and our seed all generations after us should be blessed."* (D&C 110:12)

This Elias, we understand, was the Apostle John. (See D&C 77:14)

Elder Bruce R. McConkie and others have said that John is now laboring with the lost tribes of Israel and that he will prophecy to other people yet to be revealed:

"John was translated. He has been made 'as flaming fire and a ministering angel,' and 'he shall minister for those who shall be heirs of salvation who dwell on the earth.' To him the Lord said: 'Thou shalt tarry until I come in my glory, and shalt prophesy before nations, kindreds, tongues and people.' (D&C 7:1-5.) Except for his work among the lost tribes of Israel, the 'nations, and tongues, and kings' to whom he has and shall prophesy have not yet been made known." *(Doctrinal New Testament Commentary*, Vol.3, p.508)

Joseph Fielding Smith, quoting David Whitmer, added this comment about the activities of John:

"When we see things in the Spirit and by the power of God they seem to be right here present. The signs of the times indicate the near approach of the coming forth of the other plates, but when it will be, I cannot tell. The Three Nephites are at work among the lost tribes and elsewhere. John the Revelator is at work, and I believe the time will come suddenly, before we are prepared for it." *(Life of Joseph F. Smith*, p.244)

—Gramps

DID DINOSAURS LIVE IN THE TIME OF ADAM AND EVE?

Dear Gramps,
On BBC TV, there is an animation series about dinosaurs. Must we conclude for ourselves that these pre-historic animals lived in the times of Adam and Eve in the terrestrial world or not? Otherwise, where is the logic, as Spock (startrek) would say?
Anton, from Antwerp, Belgium

Dear Anton,

It is impossible to piece together the chronology of the earth from the few statements of revealed word on the subject. However, the revealed word is truth. It is always intriguing to attempt to rationalize revealed truth with scientific evidence and theory, but this is seldom possible. There are two conflicting scientific theories on which geologic chronology is based. We can have confidence in neither because the *a priori* conditions on which they are based do not concur with revealed truth. So, we are simply left with insufficient information to answer such questions as you ask.

I would, however, add one caution. Although the scientific method is extremely practical for predicting the results of experimental conditions, scientific theory considers only telestial phenomena and cannot be expected to make valid conclusions related to non-telestial conditions. Therefore, it would seem well to accept the revealed word as truth, and where it may not concur with scientific evidence it would be well to withhold judgement until additional scientific data would concur with the revealed word.

—Gramps

WHAT DO THE SCRIPTURES MEAN ABOUT THE AARONIC PRIESTHOOD HOLDING THE KEYS OF THE MINISTERING OF ANGELS?

Dear Gramps,

When John the Baptist restored the Aaronic Priesthood to Joseph Smith and Oliver Cowdery, one of the very few instructions he gave on that priesthood was that it "holds the keys of the ministering of angels..." As one who grew up in the church and, as an adult, having worked in the Aaronic Priesthood quorums as an instructor, I have noticed that there is very little, if any, instruction given to Aaronic Priesthood holders about using the key of the ministering of angels. Do you know why this is so? Or is it just me?

Kurious in Korea

Dear Kurious in Korea,

First we should consider with whom do angels converse and to whom do they minister? It would be difficult to believe that angels approach those who are steeped in sin or who are troubled because of unworthiness. When a person has repented and is baptized he receives the Gift of the Holy Ghost. This gift is manifest only according to the righteousness of the individual. If, after baptism, that person commits further sin, the Holy Spirit withdraws and the person is left to himself until he repents and is forgiven.

The Aaronic Priesthood has the authority to administer the ordinance of baptism by which the repentant are forgiven of their sins. Being thus cleansed, they are in a position to receive the influence of the Holy Ghost and the ministering of angels. Further, the Aaronic Priesthood administers the emblems of the atonement through which the baptismal covenant is renewed and the contrite and repentant are again forgiven of their sins. Thus, the Aaronic Priesthood holds the keys to the ministering of angels by having the authority to perform those ordinances through which sin may be forgiven, and the person emerge as worthy of the guidance and direction provided by the Lord through his ministering servants.

For a thorough discussion on this subject see the October 1998 conference address of Elder Dallin H. Oaks, *Ensign*, Nov. 1998, pp. 37-39.
—Gramps

How can I keep from losing my temper?

Gramps,

I know we are supposed to love our neighbor and our enemies as ourselves. But I have found myself struggling with a person who has just joined the church and who plays one person against another where I work. This is causing comments about this person and about the church. This person seems to love causing conflict and getting people to feel sorry for her. I keep trying to love her as a sister and hate her actions, but I have found several times that she has raised my anger. What scriptures could I read to learn how to deal with this behavior and to prevent losing self control and my temper?

Harry, from Texas

Dear Harry,

Gaining self control, including controlling one's temper, is indeed a noble goal. In fact, it lies at the heart of the purpose of our existence in mortality. The Lord said,

> *And there stood one among them that was like unto God, and he said unto those who were with him: We will go down, for there is space there, and we will take of these materials, and we will make an earth whereon these may dwell; And we will prove them herewith, to see if they will do all things whatsoever the Lord their God shall command them; And they who keep their first estate shall be added upon; and they who keep not their first estate shall not have glory in the same kingdom with those who keep their first estate; and they who keep their second estate shall have glory added upon their heads for ever and ever.* (Abraham 3:24-26)

One of the principle purposes of mortality, other than gaining a body, is to gain control over that body so that it becomes subject to the will of the spirit. The Lord influences us through our spirit or our intellect. Satan influences us through our body or our emotions.

How do we gain self control? All skills are gained by practice. So, I guess one answer to your question is practice, practice, practice! If you were in an environment of all sweetness and light where nothing contrary or disturbing ever happened, you would have no opportunity for growth. Being placed in the company of one who tends to unsettle your equilibrium is actually a blessing. It provides the opportunity for the practicing of self control. In all these matters the Savior is our Great Exemplar. We are instructed,

> *Therefore I would that ye should be perfect even as I, or your Father who is in heaven is perfect.* (3 Nephi 12:48)

> *Therefore, hold up your light that it may shine unto the world. Behold I am the light which ye shall hold up—that which ye have seen me do.* (3 Nephi 18:24)

> *Then said Jesus, Father, forgive them; for they know not what they do.* (Luke 23:34)

If He forgave those who put him to death, can we not forgive those of whose actions we do not approve? Without condoning inappropriate behavior can we not show love and concern for such a person when the Savior has commanded us to

> *Love your enemies, bless them that curse you, do good to them that hate you, and pray for them which despitefully use you, and persecute you?* (Matthew 5:44)

—Gramps

DID ONE-THIRD OF THE HOSTS OF HEAVEN FOLLOW SATAN?

Gramps,

I recently went to a Know Your Religion class and the speaker said that the reference to the one-third of the hosts of Heaven who were cast out with Satan was not meant to be taken literally. He said that "one-third" meant a "part of" or a "certain amount." What do you think?

—FH

Dear FH,
I don't know. I didn't count them.
—Gramps

WHY WOULD THE SAVIOR DESTROY ENTIRE BOOK OF MORMON CITIES WITH THEIR WOMEN AND CHILDREN?

Dear Gramps,

I was stunned reading Nephi the other day where Jesus Christ destroyed entire cities, including women and children. I asked my Mormon neighbor, who rhetorically referred me to Sodom and Gomorrah. But I was shocked that the Savior of the World, the Prince of Peace, the King of Forgiveness would do such a thing. I am bitterly confused.

Chuck from Texas

Dear Chuck,

As you imply, the Savior of the world is indeed the king of forgiveness. His love for the children of God is so infinitely vast that he has taken upon himself all their sins and suffered beyond measure that they would not have to suffer if they would only listen to him, obey his word, and adopt those practices that were designed for their own happiness. Nevertheless, he is not a "namby-pamby" God, who winks at sin and demands no accountability. He has said:

> *"Therefore I command you to repent—repent, lest I smite you by the rod of my mouth, and by my wrath, and by my anger, and your sufferings be sore—how sore you know not, how exquisite you know not, yea, how hard to bear you know not. For behold, I, God, have suffered these things for all, that they might not suffer if they would repent; But if they would not repent they must suffer even as I; Which suffering caused myself, even God, the greatest of all, to tremble because of pain, and to bleed at every pore, and to suffer both body and spirit—and would that I might not drink the bitter cup, and shrink— Nevertheless, glory be to the Father, and I partook and finished my preparations unto the children of men."* (D&C 19:15-19)

Consider this scripture—by rejecting the Savior and his sacrifice, we cut ourselves off from the benefits and must suffer for our sins as if there had been no Savior. We must come to the bar of justice alone, condemned by our own actions and our own admission, and pay "the uttermost farthing" for the wicked things that we have done.

Yet there can be purpose in suffering. Hopefully, we will learn from our afflictions, that it is far better to obey the word of God. Again, Jesus said:

> *Verily I say unto you, concerning your brethren who have been afflicted, and persecuted, and cast out from the land of their inheritance— I, the Lord, have suffered the affliction to come upon them, wherewith they have been afflicted, in consequence of their transgressions; I will own them, and they shall be mine in that day when I shall come to make up my jewels. Therefore, they must needs be chastened and tried, even as Abraham, who was commanded to offer up his only son. For all those who will not endure chastening, but deny me, cannot be sanctified. Behold, I say unto you, there were jarrings, and contentions, and envyings, and strifes, and lustful and covetous desires among them; therefore by these things they polluted their inheritances. They were slow to hearken unto the voice of the Lord their God; therefore, the Lord their God is slow to hearken unto their prayers, to answer them in the day of their trouble. In the day of their peace they esteemed lightly my counsel; but, in the day of their trouble, of necessity they feel after me. Verily I say unto you, notwithstanding their sins, my bowels are filled with compassion towards them. I will not utterly cast them off; and in the day of wrath I will remember mercy. I have sworn, and the decree hath gone forth by a former commandment which I have given unto you, that I would let fall the sword of mine indignation in behalf of my people; and even as I have said, it shall come to pass. Mine indignation is soon to be poured out without measure upon all nations; and this will I do when the cup of their iniquity is full. And in that day all who are found upon the watchtower, or in other words, all mine Israel, shall be saved. And they that have been scattered shall be gathered. And all they who have mourned shall be comforted. all they who have given their lives for my name shall be crowned. Therefore, let your hearts be comforted concerning Zion; for all flesh is in mine hands; be still and know that I am God?* (D&C 101:1-16)

The destruction, of which you are concerned, occurred just prior to the advent of the Savior among the Nephites and following His resurrection. The wickedness of the people at that time was without equal:

> *Now the cause of this iniquity of the people was this—Satan had great power, unto the stirring up of the people to do all manner of iniquity, and to the puffing them up with pride, tempting them to seek for power, and authority, and riches, and the vain things of the world. And thus Satan did lead away the hearts of the people to do all manner of iniquity; therefore they had enjoyed peace but a few years. And thus, in the commencement of the thirtieth year—the people having been delivered up for the space of a long time to be carried about by the temptations of the devil whithersoever he desired to carry them, and to do whatsoever iniquity he desired they should—and thus in the commencement of this, the thirtieth year, they were in a state of awful wickedness. Now they did not sin ignorantly, for they knew the will of God concerning them, for it had been taught unto them; therefore they did wilfully rebel against God.* (3 Nephi 6:15-18)

At the coming of the resurrected Lord among the Nephites, all those rebellious people were utterly destroyed because of their wickedness. Undoubtedly there were among them innocent children who knew no sin, but were in the care of their wicked parents. Was their destruction a careless or non-caring act? Not by any means! Suppose they had been spared a quick death only to suffer a slow death in agony. Conversely, in the spirit world they were received and loved by the Savior and cared for by other loving, kind spirits. Without a doubt they would have received the blessings that the Savior gave to the little children as recorded in 3 Nephi 10:21-24:

> *And when he had said these words, he wept, and the multitude bare record of it, and he took their little children, one by one, and blessed them, and prayed unto the Father for them. And when he had done this he wept again; And he spake unto the multitude, and said unto them: Behold your little ones. And as they looked to behold they cast their eyes towards heaven, and they saw the heavens open, and they saw angels descending out of heaven as it were in the midst of fire; and they came down and encircled those little ones about, and they were encircled about with fire; and the angels did minister unto them.*

The scriptures are true. It would be well for us not to attempt to judge the Lord based on the narrow and limited perspective we have in mortality, but to believe in him, in his mercy, in his justice, and in his revealed word; then do all that we can to not rebel against the Savior of the World, the Prince of Peace, the King of Forgiveness.

—Gramps

Is the office of Branch President equivalent to that of Bishop?

Gramps,

I was listening to conference talks on my commute home today and one talk centered on bishops and their responsibilities as leaders of their particular units. My question is, other than the unit size, what is the difference between a bishop and branch president in the duties, responsibilities, keys and authority given. It is said that a bishop is a bishop for life. Is the same true for a branch president?

R. from Kansas

Dear R,

Persons called to be bishops are ordained to the office of bishop and are set apart to preside over wards in organized stakes. The bishop is the president of the Aaronic Priesthood in his ward. A person called to be a bishop is also ordained a High Priest, so that he may preside over all the members of his ward, including other High Priests. Thus, the priesthood calling of bishop is as permanent as that of Elder or High Priest.

In the mission fields, where the membership of the church has not advanced to the point where stakes may be organized, the church is organized into branches and districts. Branches and districts are normally presided over by men who hold the office of Elder in the Melchizedek Priesthood. The offices of Branch and District Presidents are assignments and are not ordinations.

Not all branch presidents have had the opportunity to go through the temple, so in the mission field, temple recommends would normally be issued by the mission president, rather than by the branch and district presidents. In some developing stakes, branch units may also be organized where there is not sufficient membership or leadership in a given location to warrant the organization of a ward.

—Gramps

What do the letters on the Kirtland Temple pulpits mean?

Dear Gramps,
What do the letters mean on the Kirtland temple pulpits? MPI and
MPC , I think.
Roger, from Thousand Oaks, California

Dear Roger,
As you know there are two sets of pulpits on each of two floors in the Kirkland Temple. Those on the west are for the presidency of the Melchizedek Priesthood and those on the east are for the presidency of the Aaronic Priesthood. The initials on the pulpits on the west refer to the following: M.P.C. (Melchizedek Presiding Council), P.M.H. (Presiding Melchizedek High Priesthood), M.H.P. (Melchizedek High Priesthood), and P.E.M. (Presiding Elder Melchizedek).

Here is an interesting description of the two sets of pulpits from the autobiography of Heber C. Kimball—

"In each of these rooms were built two pulpits, one in each end. Each pulpit consisted of four different apartments; the fourth standing on a platform raised a suitable height above the floor; the third stood directly behind and elevated a little above the fourth; the second in rear of and elevated above the third; and in like manner the first above the second. Each of these apartments was just large enough and rightly calculated to seat three persons, and the breastwork in front of each of these three last mentioned was constituted of three semi-circles joining each other, and finished in good style. The fourth or lower one, was straight in front, and had an elegant table leaf attached to it, that could be raised at pleasure for the convenience of administering the sacrament, etc. These pulpits were alike in each end of the house. One was for the use of the Melchizedek or High Priesthood, and the other for the Aaronic or lesser Priesthood. The first or highest apartment was occupied by the First Presidency over the whole church; the second apartment by the Melchizedek High Priesthood; the third by the President of the High Priests' Quorum; and the fourth by the President of the Elders and his two counselors. The highest apartment of the other pulpit was occupied by the Bishop of the church and his two counselors; the next by the President of the Priests and his two counselors; the third by the President of the Teachers and his two counselors; and the fourth by the President of the Deacons and his two counselors." (*Heber Kimball Autobiography*, Journal excerpts, p.88 - p.89)

—Gramps

ARE FAITHFUL LATTER-DAY SAINTS THE ONLY ONES WHO WILL GO TO HEAVEN?

Gramps,
I heard that Mormons believe that if you are not baptized a Mormon that you won't be able to go to heaven. Is that true? Also, I've heard that Mormons believe that if you are sealed in the temple, you will becomes gods and goddesses in the afterlife. Is that also true?
Ashley, from Nevada

Dear Ashley,
No, idea that LDS people feel that they are the only ones who will go to heaven is a false concept that is often circulated about Latter-day Saints and it stems from a misconception about the doctrine of the Church of Jesus Christ of Latter-day Saints. Let's see if we can clear the issue up a bit.

The sectarian world believes, in general, that there is only one heaven and one hell with an indefinite line (depending on whose opinion you accept on criteria of righteousness) dividing the two. My understanding is (and I may be as much in error about sectarian doctrine as the sectarians are about LDS doctrine) that all those who meet some minimum set of criteria of righteousness and/or comply with certain dogma (again, open to interpretation) will be saved and go to heaven. They will be joined together in righteousness, forgiven of their sins, and reign with Christ in eternity. All those who fail to meet the minimum criteria of righteousness will be consigned in misery to a never-ending hell under the domination of Satan.

The Church of Jesus Christ of Latter-day Saints believes, as taught by Paul in 1 Cor.15:40-41, that in the heavens there are three degrees of glory. Let me quote the scripture, because it needs a little explanation.

> *There are also celestial bodies, and bodies terrestrial: but the glory of the celestial is one, and the glory of the terrestrial is another. There is one glory of the sun, and another glory of the moon, and another glory of the stars: for one star differeth from another star in glory.* (1 Cor.15:40-41)

Paul mentions only two degrees of glory—the celestial and the terrestrial. However, in the immediate comparison with astronomical bodies, he mentions three—the sun, the moon and the stars. Actually, part of the original verse 40 is missing. When Joseph Smith translated the Bible, he gave 1 Cor. 15:40 as follows:

> *Also celestial bodies, and bodies terrestrial, and bodies telestial; but the glory of the celestial, one; and the terrestrial, another; and the telestial, another.*

which clarifies that the three degrees of glory are the celestial (compared to the sun), the terrestrial (compared to the moon) and the telestial (compared to the stars).

The Church of Jesus Christ of Latter-day Saints teaches that the only ones who will not inherit one of these three degrees of glory are the son of perdition. It is only those sons of perdition who will be lost to Satan and will live with him in misery for eternity. So you see, the Latter-day Saints are much more generous than the rest of Christianity in their belief of who is going to heaven.

Now a word of explanation about who will inherit these three degrees of glory, from which you will be able to perceive the source of the Protestant error in its interpretation of LDS beliefs.

Those who will inherit the lowest of the three degrees of glory, the telestial heaven, are identified in the Doctrine and Covenants as follows:

> *For these are they who are of Paul, and of Apollos, and of Cephas. These are they who say they are some of one and some of another—some of Christ and some of John, and some of Moses, and some of Elias, and some of Esaias, and some of Isaiah, and some of Enoch; But received not the gospel, neither the testimony of Jesus, neither the prophets, neither the everlasting covenant. Last of all,*

these all are they who will not be gathered with the saints, to be caught up unto the church of the Firstborn, and received into the cloud. These are they who are liars, and sorcerers, and adulterers, and whoremongers, and whosoever loves and makes a lie. These are they who suffer the wrath of God on earth. These are they who suffer the vengeance of eternal fire. These are they who are cast down to hell and suffer the wrath of Almighty God, until the fulness of times, when Christ shall have subdued all enemies under his feet, and shall have perfected his work; When he shall deliver up the kingdom, and present it unto the Father, spotless, saying: I have overcome and have trodden the wine-press alone, even the wine-press of the fierceness of the wrath of Almighty God. (D&C 76:99-107)

These are the wicked people of the earth who will pay the full price for their own sins, since they refused to accept the great atoning sacrifice of the Savior. Therefore, as mentioned above, they will be cast down to hell and will live in misery with Satan during the thousand years of the Millennium. Then, after having paid to the demands of justice the full price for all their sins, they will be redeemed, resurrected, and will inherit the glory of the telestial kingdom, which glory is far greater than we can imagine. The scriptures state:

And thus we saw, in the heavenly vision, the glory of the telestial, <u>which surpasses all understanding</u>. (D&C 76:89)

Those who will inherit the higher terrestrial glory of heaven are the good people of the earth, but who nevertheless do not accept the Savior as their God nor do they live according to the precepts of his gospel. Concerning them, the scriptures reveal the following:

And again, we saw the terrestrial world, and behold and lo, these are they who are of the terrestrial, whose glory differs from that of the church of the Firstborn who have received the fulness of the Father, even as that of the moon differs from the sun in the firmament. Behold, these are they who died without law; And also they who are the spirits of men kept in prison, whom the Son visited, and preached the gospel unto them, that they might be judged according to men in the flesh; Who received not the testimony of Jesus in the flesh, but afterwards received it. These are they who are honorable men of the earth, who were blinded by the craftiness of men. (D&C 76:71-75)

As opposed to the fate of the wicked, these good people of the earth are resurrected at the beginning of the Millennium and live with Christ on earth during His thousand-year millennial reign. They will then inherit a terrestrial glory. This glory will be so much greater than the telestial glory that it is compared with the telestial kingdom as the light of the moon is compared to the light from the stars.

Finally, there is the celestial glory, compared to the sun, that is defined in the scriptures as follows:

> *And again we bear record—or we saw and heard, and this is the testimony of the gospel of Christ concerning them who shall come forth in the resurrection of the just— They are they who received the testimony of Jesus, and believed on his name and were baptized after the manner of his burial, being buried in the water in his name, and this according to the commandment which he has given— by keeping the commandments they might be washed and cleansed from all their sins, and receive the Holy Spirit by the laying on of the hands of him who is ordained and sealed unto this power; And who overcome by faith, and are sealed by the Holy Spirit of promise, which the Father sheds forth upon all those who are just and true. They are they who are the church of the Firstborn. They are they into whose hands the Father has given all things— They are they who are priests and kings, who have received of his fulness, and of his glory; And are priests of the Most High, after the order of Melchizedek, which was after the order of Enoch, which was after the order of the Only Begotten Son. Wherefore, as it is written, they are gods, even the sons of God— Wherefore, all things are theirs, whether life or death, or things present, or things to come, all are theirs and they are Christ's, and Christ is God's.* (D&C 76:50-59)

Latter-day Saints believe that The Church of Jesus Christ of Latter-day Saints is actually the established kingdom of God on the earth. It is presided over by Jesus Christ, who directs its operation through revelation to holy men whom He has called as His prophets. God's authority to administer the ordinances of salvation has been given to and resides with this body. Those who accept the Savior as their God, and who faithfully obey all his commandments, including receiving all the saving ordinances of the gospel, will inherit the celestial glory, *where God and Christ dwell.* (D&C 76:112)

The second part of your question, about gods and goddesses, is answered in the above scripture. The statement made above, *Wherefore, as it is written, they are gods, even the sons of God*, cites an earlier scripture. Paul refers to the same concept in 1 Cor. 8:5-6, where he says—

> *For though there be that are called gods, whether in heaven or in earth, (as there be gods many, and lords many), But to us there is but one God, the Father, of whom are all things, and we in him; and one Lord Jesus Christ, by whom are all things, and we by him.*

Thus, those who live by every word that proceeds forth from the mouth of God (Matthew 4:4) will become gods in eternity, and as Paul says, will continue to worship God the Father, and his Son Jesus Christ.
—Gramps

WHICH CHURCH IS THE GREAT AND ABOMINABLE CHURCH?

Gramps,

I teach Gospel Doctrine and today's lesson was about Nephi's vision of the "great and abominable church." I made it clear by reading quotes from others and from the manual that this "church" does reference any one church in particular. I explained that basically it refers to all churches that do not teach the full truth. Most everyone in class seemed to disagree saying that it refers to the Catholic Church since all other churches, for the most part, branch off from it. I thought you could clarify it a little more.

Donna, from Indiana

Dear Donna,

Let's look carefully at the scriptures. It's important that we accept what they say and that we not attempt to impose our private interpretations on them. We read in 1 Nephi 14:10 that there are save two churches only. If someone were to name the Catholic Church as the great and abominable, what about all the others? Are they therefore not churches? Nonsense! When the Lord says that there are two churches only, He is not speaking of the man made religious organizations, as they comprise many churches. All of these churches do much good.

They may not have the authority or the necessary doctrine to assure either salvation or exaltation in the celestial kingdom. But their practitioners, through adherence to their churches' beliefs and through living good lives, are assured by the Lord to inherit kingdoms of glory. Hugh Nibley has offered this insight:

> "Now we have 'that great pit, which hath been digged for them by that 'great and abominable church.' You notice that the great and abominable church is not capitalized. It's not one particular institution. I think that may be significant that the brethren left it that way." (Hugh Nibley, *Teachings of the Book of Mormon*, Semester 1, p.202)

In the scripture you cite the Lord is not speaking of the organized churches as we know them. One church in that scripture is the Church of the Lamb of God and the other is the church of the devil. We might begin by asking, What is the Church of the Lamb of God? In verse 12 we read that "the Church of the Lamb, who were the saints of God." So the Church of the Lamb is composed of the saints of God. Next, we ask, Who are the saints of God? Again, the answer is given in this same chapter. Verse 14 says,

> *And it came to pass that I, Nephi, beheld the power of the Lamb of God, that it descended upon the saints of the church of the Lamb, and upon the covenant people of the Lord.*

The word "and" here does not mean "and also," it means "and in other words." This phrase is a synonymous parallelism, with which the scriptures are replete, meaning that the saints of the Church of the Lamb are the covenant people of the Lord.

Who then are the covenant people of the Lord? They are those who, in the holy temples, make sacred covenants of obedience to the gospel and who live by their covenants. Not every member of the Church of Jesus Christ of Latter-day Saints has made and keeps the covenants of the holy temple. So I hope that I will not be misunderstood if I say that the Church of Jesus Christ of Latter-day Saints is not the Church of the Lamb. However, let us quickly add that it is the guardian of the covenants of the Church of the Lamb. It may be that not all the members of the Church of Jesus Christ of Latter-day Saints are of the Church of the Lamb, but all of the members of the Church of the Lamb are indeed faithful members of the Church of Jesus Christ of Latter-day Saints.

The scriptures tell us that

> *whoso belongeth not to the church of the Lamb of God belongeth to that great church, which is the mother of abominations...*

This statement helps define the two churches. It is apparent that they go far beyond the manmade organizations of today. Every person in every age of the world who has made and keeps the sacred covenants of salvation, who has had his garments washed clean in the blood of the Lamb, who has been sanctified from sin, is of the Church of the Lamb of God. All others are influenced to one degree or another by the Adversary of all righteousness. Elder B.H. Roberts settled this question in his *Defense of the Faith and the Saints*, Vol. 1, p.31:

> "I would not like, therefore, to designate the Catholic Church as the church of the devil. Neither would I like to designate any one or all of the various divisions and subdivisions of Protestant Christendom combined as such church; nor the Greek Catholic Church; nor the Buddhist sects; nor the followers of Confucius; nor the followers of Mohammed; nor would I like to designate even the societies formed by deists and atheists as constituting the church of the devil. The Book of Mormon text ought to be read in connection with its context"

—Gramps

WHY IS IT WRONG TO PLAY WITH OUIJA BOARDS?

Dear Gramps,

My son asked me why it is wrong to play with Ouija boards. He is only seven. How can I explain to him why we don't play with these things? I would really like to give him a reason that he could under-stand. Any suggestions?

CC

Dear CC,

You might tell him that people who use Ouija boards are trying to make contact with the spirit world and that the only spirits who would consider responding to such a thing are the bad spirits.

God has already given us a way to contact the spirit world. He tells us that we should talk only with Him and that we don't need any kind of a mechanism to do so because He hears every word that we say. If we talk to our Heavenly Father, really believing that He is there, He will answer our prayers according to His perfect love and kindness toward His children.

One of our hymns treats this subject:
Prayer is the simplest form of speech
That infant lips can try,
Prayer, the sublimest strains that reach
The Majesty on high.

—Gramps

How do I help prepare my boyfriend for a mission?

Dear Gramps,

I have been a member of the church for about two years now, and I was introduced to the gospel by the young man I have been dating for three years. At the time we met (my freshman year in college and his sophomore year), my boyfriend (let's call him Ray) was actually having a bit of a faith crisis, but as I questioned him more about his church, he began to bear his testimony in small bits and pieces, and it eventually grew. After about a year of thorough investigating on my part (and a lot of patience on the part of Ray), I joined the church. I can honestly say it's been the most beneficial decision I've ever made.

Ray has now decided to go on a mission, and I'm thrilled for him. I think he'll be a great missionary, and I also think I need some time to spend on my own before I can become someone's eternal companion.

As the time for him to leave draws closer, I find myself concerned that our relationship may distract him from adequately preparing. We are geographically separated at present (because he is student teaching), which has provided us with the opportunity to date other people (and we had agreed that it would be a good idea), but so far that hasn't happened. I live in an area that has relatively few YSA, and the YSA elders from my branch seem to be, well, not interested in me. I also wonder if the fact that Ray and I have dated for so long has branded me as "off-limits."

I have two questions: 1) How can I help Ray prepare to serve an honorable mission? 2) What do you suggest I do in terms of dating other people?

Kelly, New York State

Dear Kelly,

The power of a good companion is underappreciated. The value of a righteous woman, who helps a young man prepare to be a servant of the Lord, is inestimable. You are probably largely responsible for Ray's decision to adhere to the principles of the gospel and to serve the Lord as a missionary. Your insistence on the highest moral integrity and your encouraging Ray to serve as a missionary will probably be key factors in his continued preparation.

I would be careful, however, about any long-term promises to remain committed to one another. When Ray returns from his mission he will not be the same person that he was when he left. Neither will you. You might promise to write to him during his mission and that would be a good thing. But I would suggest that promises of any permanent relationship would be better deferred until you renew your relationship after his mission, and see how you feel about each other at that time.

Concerning your second question, if you have had a rather steady relationship with Ray, you have sent a "hands-off" signal to the rest of the young men. They would not want to encroach on Ray's territory, and they would also probably fear being rejected if they were to ask you for a date. So if you were to let it be known that you entertain no ideas of a permanent relationship and participate in the group social functions, you will no doubt announce your availability to the other young men.

—Gramps

WHERE DID THE TERM 'TAILGATE' COME FROM?

Gramps,
The other day as we were driving someone decided that they wanted to tailgate us. I know that this is not an odd occurrence, but we were just wondering if you could tell us how the term 'tailgate' came about?
Jason

Dear Jason,

The term 'tailgate' actually refers to a board or gate at the rear of a vehicle that can be removed or let down, as for loading. The term was first used in 1868 as it applied to wagons, such as delivery wagons. So tailgating is a logical term implying driving too close to the tailgate of a vehicle—even those without tailgates. I suppose the term could have been called 'bumpering' if it had come into vogue after the invention of the automobile. Indeed, many early pickup trucks had no bumpers, as that would have interfered with loading and unloading.

As early as 1965, the term 'tailgate' began to be used in connection with a party that was set up on the tailgate of a station wagon. Tailgate parties now refer to parties that accompany a sporting event.

—Gramps

WHY IS THE TEMPLE FILM SEQUENCE OF THE CREATION NOT THE SAME AS THE ACCOUNT IN GENESIS?

Dear Gramps,
Can you tell me why the account in Genesis states what happened on each creation day differently than the temple film?
—Loretta, from Sandy, Utah

Dear Loretta,

There are five accounts in the scriptures that detail the sequence of the organization of the earth–Genesis 1, Moses 2 and 3, and Abraham 4 and 5. Genesis 1, Moses 2, and Abraham 4 are consistent with each other in the sequence of the creation. Both Moses 3 and Abraham 5, however, specify that these scriptures refer to a spiritual creation, or the planning phase. For instance, we read the following in Moses 3:4-5:

> *And now, behold, I say unto you, that these are the generations of the heaven and of the earth, when they were created, in the day that I, the Lord God, made the heaven and the earth, And<u>every plant of the field before it was in the earth, and every herb of the field before it grew</u>. For <u>I, the Lord God, created all things, of which I have spoken, spiritually, before they were naturally upon the face of the earth</u>. For I, the Lord God, had not caused it to rain upon the face of the earth. And <u>I, the Lord God, had created all the children of men; and not yet a man to till the ground; for in heaven created I them; and there was not yet flesh upon the earth, neither in the water, neither in the air.</u>*

And in Abraham 5:1-3, the Gods conclude that they will do what they had *planned* to do. In fact, the heading to Abraham 5 says,

> *The Gods finish their planning of the creation of all things—They bring to pass the creation according to their plans."*

The physical creation happened in a different order than the spiritual creation. In the spiritual creation, man was created *after* the plants and animals; in the physical creation he was created *before* the plants and animals. The temple sequence follows the creation account given in Genesis 1, Moses 2, and Abraham 4.

Another account of the creation sequence was given by Brigham Young, as follows:

"Though we have it in history that our father Adam was made of the dust of this earth, and that he knew nothing about his God previous to being made here, yet it is not so; and when we learn the truth we shall see and understand that he helped to make this world, and was the chief manager in that operation. He was the person who brought the animals and the seeds from other planets to this world, and brought a wife with him and stayed here. You may read and believe what you please as to what is found written in the Bible. Adam was made from the dust of an earth, but not from the dust of this earth. He was made as you and I are made, and no person was ever made upon any other principle." *(Journal of Discourses,* Vol.3, p.319)

So we see from Brigham Young that both scriptural accounts are correct. Consistent with Moses3:7-22, Adam was placed on the earth *before* the plants and animals because he brought them here as one of those who helped form and prepare the earth. He then returned to take up permanent residence and brought with him his wife, consistent with Moses 3:21-22.

—Gramps

HOW CAN I HONOR MY MOTHER,
WHO OPPOSES MY BELIEFS?

Dear Gramps,

My husband, children, and I converted to the gospel five years ago. My father is respectful of our decision, but my mother is against everything we believe in, and we cannot even mention anything about the church or state our beliefs without her becoming rude and hysterical. She, of course, would like to influence our children. How can I honor my mother?

Julie, from Washington

Dear Julie,

You can honor your mother by respecting her, showing that you love her, doing things with her, and being as agreeable as possible. If she is upset by your religious beliefs, then that would not be an appropriate topic for discussion. She must know by now that you and your family are sincere in your beliefs. If she brings up the subject of your beliefs in a conversation, you would certainly be justified in defending them. But you could refuse to enter into a discussion that would be upsetting to you or your mother.

Without a doubt, the example of your faithfulness to your own beliefs will have its impact for good, and the time may well come when your mother could change her mind. It would be important to pray for her every day, asking the Lord to soften her heart toward the things of the Kingdom. Miracles occur daily.

—Gramps

WAS THE SAVIOR CRUCIFIED ON A THURSDAY OR A FRIDAY?

Dear Gramps,
Was the Savior crucified on a Thursday or Friday? I think it was a Thursday. Some say Friday. Any thoughts on this?.
Roger, from Brea, California

Dear Roger,

The Savior was crucified on a Friday. We may know this from the following information: It was customary for Jews, during the period between Paschal week and Pentecost, to fast twice a week—on Mondays and Thursdays. These days were chosen because, according to tradition, Moses went up to Mount Sinai to receive the Tables of the Law on a Thursday and came down again on a Monday. (See Bruce R. McConkie, *The Mortal Messiah*, Vol.1, pp.184-85)

When the Jews had determined to kill Jesus, they would not have it to be on the fast day for fear of causing an uproar among the people.

> *And it came to pass, when Jesus had finished all these sayings, he said unto his disciples, Ye know that after two days is the feast of the passover, and the Son of man is betrayed to be crucified. Then assembled together the chief priests, and the scribes, and the elders of the people, unto the palace of the high priest, who was called Caiaphas, And consulted that they might take Jesus by subtilty, and kill him. But they said, <u>Not on the feast day, lest there be an uproar among the people</u>.*(Matthew 26:1-6)

The fasts were from sundown to sundown, so the Savior invited the Twelve to break the fast with him on the evening of that fateful Thursday.

> *And in the evening he cometh with the twelve. And as they sat and did eat, Jesus said, Verily I say unto you, One of you which eateth with me shall betray me…And when they had sung an hymn, they went out into the mount of Olives.* (Mark 14:18-19,26)

The Savior, betrayed by Judas, was taken captive that night, and on the following day, Friday, he was crucified.

—Gramps

WAS JOSEPH SMITH A WEALTHY MAN?

Gramps,

I am always arguing with my mother about The Book of Mormon and other LDS issues. She is a not a member and tries to prove that Joseph Smith was a fraud and that the whole church is a fraud. I love her arguing because it makes my testimony stronger every day. Last night I had a dream that we were arguing about Joseph Smith and she told me he was in it for the money and that was the only reason he conned every one. I told her that he wasn't in it for the money. I said "He was born a poor man and he died a poor man." After waking up this morning I could not believe how real the conversation seemed. But I keep questioning my dream. Did he live and die a poor man? I am not sure if he did. But if he did then I will be calling my mother to let her know.

Jesse

Dear Jesse,

The Prophet Joseph was in no way a wealthy man. He had only three years of formal schooling because of the necessity of working to help support his family. He was told by the Lord in a revelation that gaining wealth was not his strength. He was told that

> *in temporal labors thou shalt not have strength, for this is not thy calling.* (D&C 24:9)

He was in debt at the time of his death. In fact, In January 1851 a judgement was entered against his heirs requiring foreclosure on the property that he had owned in order to pay off his debts. (Dallin H. Oaks and Joseph I. Bentley, *BYU Studies,* Vol. 19)

—Gramps

HOW COME I DON'T FEEL THE SPIRIT WHEN I GO TO THE TEMPLE?

Dear Gramps,

I have not discussed this with anyone, but I do not feel about the temple like everyone I know. I have been to get my endowments, etc., but I do not feel "the spirit" there and find the ceremonies strange and confusing. I am not married to a member and sometimes I feel that maybe I am subconsciously not feeling anything because I cannot have the "eternal marriage." I don't have any desire to go to the temple or sit in church listening to all the temple talks and how the members feel when they go. I am the only one who feels like this?

BC

Dear BC,

I doubt very much that you are alone in your feelings, but let's try to address your concerns one at a time. The temple ceremonies may indeed seem strange when compared with what we know and experience in the outside world. But each part of each ceremony has a specific meaning and significance. The eternal truths that God reveals to His children in the holy temples must be represented in some manner.

The important thing is not the manner of representation but what the representation stands for. We live in a world of symbols. The symbols of one society or culture would indeed seem strange to those of another. Let's look at just a couple of examples.

In some early Polynesian cultures, when a couple married, they made a cut in the wrist of one arm of each partner, then tied the arms together so that the blood would mix and that they would then be "of one blood." That act would seem strange to us, but it symbolized a sacred concept to those who practiced it.

Let's say that you took out an insurance policy. You would sign your name at the bottom of the form indicating your agreement to pay the premiums. The form, printed by the insurance company, would state the conditions under which you would be indemnified. Your name at the bottom of the form is a symbol. It means much more than identifying who you are. It represents in a legally binding way your commitment to honor your promise to pay. If you default on your premiums and break your promise to pay, the insurance company is under no obligation to indemnify you for any condition stated in the policy. In fact, when you do not comply, the policy becomes null and void. However, if you do comply, the insurance company is legally bound to indemnify you according to the terms of the policy.

So it is with the symbols and the covenants that they represent in the temple. We should look beyond the symbols to the eternal verities that they represent. The truths revealed in the temple were given by revelation, and they can best be understood by the spirit of revelation. As we prayerfully seek to understand the significance of the endowment, the Lord will reveal to us *precept upon precept, here a line and there a line*, the deep meanings of the eternal truths that are available there for us to learn.

Please do not give up hope of having an eternal marriage. If you humbly and sincerely live according to the principles that you have espoused, every promise made to you in the temple will be fulfilled. How much more should we trust in the word of the Lord than in the promises of even the most reliable insurance company! In our family, my father was not a member of the church. He was a good, honorable man whom I and my sisters and our mother loved dearly, but he would have nothing to do with the church—until he was sixty-four years old. One day, out of the blue, he asked if he could be baptized. What a thrill it was to see my father become a member of the church after all those years! He passed away just a few months later.

I can't promise you that every person will react to the prayers of others as did my father, but I know this—if we do our part in living righteously, the Lord will surely bless us in the way that will be for our best good. We read in D&C 98:3,

> *Therefore, he giveth this promise unto you, with an immutable covenant that they shall be fulfilled; and all things wherewith you have been afflicted shall work together for your good, and to my names' glory, saith the Lord.*

—Gramps

WILL VARIOUS RELIGIOUS GROUPS EXIST IN THE CELESTIAL KINGDOM?

Dear Gramps,

In our High Priests class, whenever the subject of the celestial kingdom comes up, two brethren always make mention of a Joseph Smith statement they are supposed to have read that says we will be surprised to find there, Catholics, Methodists, Muslims, etc., who inherit because they lived their lives in an acceptable way.

I have gone through many books of Joseph's writings and sermons, and have found no such statement, nor would I expect to as this seems against the scriptures and statements of the general authorities. Your help please.

David, from England

Dear David,

I would suggest that you ask these two brethren to produce the statement that they are supposed to have read. If they can't produce it, their statements should be discounted. If they can produce, then I, and I assume the rest of the church, would be very much surprised. I don't wonder that you cannot find such statements by the Prophet. All that he and the other Brethren have taught is contrary to such a notion.

There are many good, just, and honorable people among the various religions of the world, as well as among those who profess no religion. They will be blessed by a kind and loving Father in Heaven for their goodness. Nothing that they have merited by their good works will be withheld from them. However, unless they repent of their erroneous concepts and submit themselves to the doctrines and the ordinances and covenants of the gospel of Jesus Christ, they are destined to enjoy only the blessings of the terrestrial kingdom and that will be the end of their glory. Where God and Christ are, they cannot come, worlds without end.

President Joseph F. Smith spoke clearly on the subject of the requirements to gain our Father's presence in these words:

"Having thus repented, the next thing requisite is baptism, which is an essential principle of the gospel—no man can enter into the gospel covenant without it. It is the door of the Church of Christ, we cannot get in there in any other way, for Christ hath said it, 'sprinkling,' or 'pouring,' is not baptism. Baptism means immersion in water, and is to be administered by one having authority, in the name of the Father, and of the Son, and of the Holy Ghost. Baptism without divine authority is not valid. It is a symbol of the burial and resurrection of Jesus Christ, and must be done in the likeness thereof, by one commissioned of God, in the manner prescribed, otherwise it is illegal and will not be accepted by Him, nor will it effect a remission of sins, the object for which it is designed, but whosoever hath faith, truly repents and is 'buried with Christ in baptism,' by one having divine authority, shall receive a remission of sins, and is entitled to the gift of the Holy Ghost by the laying on of hands." (*Gospel Doctrine,* p.101)

And President John Taylor, specifically addressed the proponents of sectarianism, stating that they are "not near the celestial kingdom."

"The Methodists, for instance, could not for a moment suppose that John Wesley was not competent to judge all matters pertaining to salvation. Wesleyan ministers will hardly permit his doctrines to be questioned; they must be swallowed without investigation. In fact, I have heard some of them say that he was a man of such erudition, talent, and piety that they would not have his doctrines questioned in their hearing. The Protestant Germans and a great many others are just the same with regard to Luther; yet in some of his ideas and principles the great Reformer was as foolish as any other man. The Scotch are a good deal so with John Knox; they think that he was everything good, praiseworthy, and amiable, and, in fact, that he was the pink of perfection. The Roman Catholics will not for a moment admit that they are not the true church; and they will maintain that they have held the keys of the Kingdom of Heaven from the days of Peter until now, and that they still have the pure doctrines of the Gospel, and have power to bind on earth and in Heaven, and to loose on earth and in Heaven. You may ask a great many who have seceded from the Church of Rome, and you would find that they have similar ideas about their own infallibility, only they are a little better than those from whom they seceded; they have made some improvements and are a little nearer the celestial kingdom." (*Journal of Discourses*, Vol.13, p.13)

—Gramps

DID EARLIER EDITIONS OF THE PEARL OF GREAT PRICE MENTION NINE-FOOT TALL GIANTS LIVING ON THE MOON?

Dear Gramps,

A friend of mine told me a story that she believes to be fact. The story goes like this: An older version of The Pearl of Great Price spoke about nine-foot tall giants who lived on our moon. When the astronauts went to the moon and found no living thing on the moon, the Mormons had to change the book. The church sent out the missionaries from all over the world to every book store, library, and any place there was a copy of The Pearl of Great Price, and the missionaries replaced all of the books with a new version that didn't mention the moon giants.

Is this a local story, or is this a common belief of all Fundamentalist Baptists? How could anyone, regardless of religion, believe a story as silly as this? Have you ever heard anything similar to this story?

Bob

Dear Bob,

If prizes were given out for ridiculous tales, I think this one would be in the running for first place. The only redeeming value of such trash is that it reveals the character of the perpetrators. They know that they are lying, and unless their stupidity would also rank in the running for first place, they also know that any rational person would recognize them for what they are. Their barbs are less than a bee-bee gun against a tank.

Do you think that such a tale would ever be propagated against any other religion than the Church of Jesus Christ of Latter-day Saints? The reason is obvious and is one of the many demonstrations that support the fact that the Church of Jesus Christ of Latter-day Saints is indeed the Kingdom of God on the earth. Although Satan is against all good and all truth, I imagine that he is not nearly as interested in discrediting a manmade religion that is without the power to exalt men and women in eternity as he is in attempting to discredit God's own earthly organization.

—Gramps

WHO WILL SAVE AMERICA?

Gramps,
Who will save America? I have heard it stated that the Latter-day Saints will be the ones to save America. Is this statement true?
CJ

Dear CJ,

You are probably referring to the statement made by Joseph Smith and recorded by Brigham Young, as follows:

"Will the Constitution be destroyed? No; it will be held inviolate by this people; and, as Joseph Smith said, 'The time will come when the destiny of the nation will hang upon a single thread. At this critical juncture, this people will step forth and save it from the threatened destruction." *(Discourses of Brigham Young, p.469)*

By the word, "people," the Prophet was referring to the members of the church. This becomes more obvious from the words of President Ezra Taft Benson, who said,

> "The Lord told the Prophet Joseph Smith there would be an attempt to overthrow the country by destroying the Constitution. Joseph Smith predicted that the time would come when the Constitution would hang, as it were, by a thread, and at that time 'this people will step forth and save it from the threatened destruction.' *(Journal of Discourses*, 7:15) It is my conviction that the elders of Israel, widely spread over the nation, will at that crucial time successfully rally the righteous of our country and provide the necessary balance of strength to save the institutions of constitutional government." *(Teachings of Ezra Taft Benson*, p.618-619)

—Gramps

SHOULD I BE CONCERNED WITH MY ABILITY TO SEE WHAT OTHERS CANNOT?

Dear Gramps,

Since the age of two I have experienced many things that the 'world' would classify as 'paranormal.' I have seen spirits many times and even heard a choir of angels. My mother and sister also have heard this. We were cleaning our ward building and went to find out who was there. When we opened the door to the Relief Society room, the music stopped, we realized we had interrupted, excused ourselves, and went about our business.

I have always been open to the fact that I have an ability to 'see' what others don't. There has only been one time when the sprits had an evil feeling about them and I was given a blessing. I have had glimpses into the future. I knew the exact moment my father passed away, for example. The list goes on. The whole thing is getting very tiring. I am very active in the church and have a strong testimony. I guess all this leads up to the question, should I be concerned with this 'ability' to see what others cannot? How open should I be in talking to others about this? I just recently told my husband of ten years. I had said bits and

pieces and then one day I just let it all out. He told me I should consider it a gift, but to be careful, and prayerful. But I am getting very weary. 'Knowing' things beforehand is very difficult, because I don't know if I should tell a person something that I know about them, or just let it go. My mind gets tired with all the information constantly flowing in. I guess I am asking an impartial person to get another insight.
K.

Dear K.

All have not every gift given unto them; for there are many gifts, and to every man is given a gift by the Spirit of God. To some is given one, and to some is given another, that all may be profited thereby. To some it is given by the Holy Ghost to know that Jesus Christ is the Son of God, and that he was crucified for the sins of the world. To others it is given to believe on their words, that they also might have eternal life if they continue faithful. And again, to some it is given by the Holy Ghost to know the differences of administration, as it will be pleasing unto the same Lord, according as the Lord will, suiting his mercies according to the conditions of the children of men. And again, it is given by the Holy Ghost to some to know the diversities of operations, whether they be of God, that the manifestations of the Spirit may be given to every man to profit withal. And again, verily I say unto you, to some is given, by the Spirit of God, the word of wisdom. To another is given the word of knowledge, that all may be taught to be wise and to have knowledge. And again, to some it is given to have faith to be healed; And to others it is given to have faith to heal. And again, to some is given the working of miracles; And to others it is given to prophesy; And to others the discerning of spirits. And again, it is given to some to speak with tongues; And to another is given the interpretation of tongues. And all these gifts come from God, for the benefit of the children of God. (D&C 46:11-26)

It appears that your wise husband could have been referring to the word of the Lord in the scripture quoted above. He seems to be understanding and loving, and has given you some good counsel.

You have an ability not enjoyed by all. But others have abilities not enjoyed by you. The gifts of the spirit with which you have been blessed have also been given to numbers of other people. I am not one of them, but some members of my wife's family have been so blessed.

You seem to be troubled by how to use these unusual abilities. First, you might consider that they are gifts of the spirit. As such, they have been given to you *for the benefit of the children of God*. If this is so, rather than being troubled you should be thankful.

You also seem concerned with how to use your gift. I might offer a few suggestions. First, some general principles: God's kingdom on the earth is governed under the direction and inspiration of priesthood authority. If you receive any impressions that are contrary to the scriptures, to the pronouncements of the Brethren, or to any local priesthood leaders, you may recognize that these particular impressions are not from the Lord and should be rejected out of hand. I would imagine, however, that the nature of your insights have more to do with individuals and their concerns rather than with doctrinal or procedural matters.

If your insights put you in a position to help others in any way, you would have a special opportunity to bless their lives. Here is where great tact and judgement should be exercised. It would probably be a good idea not to reveal the source of your knowledge. First, many won't believe it; secondly, some may look upon you as some kind of an authority and tend to swing their allegiance from God's official representatives to another source of inspiration. There could be a strong tendency to do so on the part of people of weak faith. So you might look on your gift as a guide for your own life and as an opportunity to bless the lives of others. However, you might consider the gift so sacred that you would not reveal it others. I pray that the Lord may continue to bless you, to give you peace of mind, and to point the way for the reasonable, appropriate, and practical application of your special abilities.

—Gramps

DID JESUS EVER TRAVEL TO INDIA AND BRITAIN?

Dear Gramps,
Do you have any information on the validity of the Savior's traveling the world with Joseph of Arimethia, who was a tin trader? And of

the Savior's showing up in India and Britain before his ministry started? Was his family wealthy?
Rick, from Arizona

Dear Rick,

There is a legendary account that Joseph of Arimethia was a distant relative of the family of Jesus and that he derived his wealth from tin mines in Cornwall, which he visited from time to time. The legend continues that Jesus, as a teenager, accompanied Joseph on one such visit. Based on that legendary account, William Blake (1757-1827) wrote the following poem:

And did those feet in ancient time walk upon England's mountains green?
And was the holy Lamb of God on England's pleasant pastures seen?
And did the countenance divine shine forth upon our clouded hills?
And was Jerusalem builded here among those dark satanic mills?
Bring me my bow of burning gold!
Bring me my arrows of desire!
Bring me my spear! O clouds, unfold!
Bring me my chariot of fire!
I will not cease from mental fight, nor shall my sword sleep in my hand,
Till we have built Jerusalem in England's green and pleasant land.

It was Joseph of Arimethia who was reputed to be wealthy, rather than the family of Jesus, although legend has it that Joseph was a distant cousin of Jesus.

In terms of the Savior's visiting India, that story may have come from a Hindu religion belief that a person by the name of Apollonius was the reincarnate of Jesus. Jesus is reputed by the Hindus to have lived from 24 BC to 9 AD, and Apollonius of Tyana from 16 AD to about 97 AD. He was born and died in India.

—Gramps

WHY SHOULD MORMONS BELIEVE IN JOSEPH SMITH?

Gramps,
Have you ever seen Satan? Have you ever seen God or Jesus? If
you are honest, you will answer, "No." I have to ask myself whether or
not Mormons should believe in Joseph Smith. The church doesn't like
to talk about it, but I think he did have a reputation for telling tall tales.
Why should Mormons believe him?
M.J.

Dear M.J.,
Many derogatory things have been said about the Prophet, Joseph
Smith. As a matter of fact, he was told by the Angel Moroni, <u>whom he
saw</u>,

> *that* [his] *name should be had for good and evil among all*
> *nations, kindreds, and tongues, or that it should be both good and evil*
> *spoken of among all people.* (Joseph Smith—History 1:33)

If I were you, I would check my sources very carefully before I
subscribed to such derogatory comments about the Prophet.
There are millions of Mormons who not only believe that Joseph
Smith actually saw God the Father and his Son Jesus Christ, but who
have themselves received witnesses from God that the Prophet actually
did see them. You, too, can personally come to know these things and
receive a true witness from the Father if you sincerely desire to know
rather than trying in a vain to prove that they are not so.
—Gramps

SHOULD CHURCH LEADERS BE TRULY WORTHY AND LIVE EXEMPLARY LIVES?

Gramps,
On the question of inspiration to call leaders who may not be truly honest or worthy in their lives, shouldn't they be able to use their calling as an opportunity to repent? If they don't correct themselves or until they do, are they worthy temple recommend holders? If they are not worthy, is the temple desecrated by their patronage?
Anonymous, from Oklahoma

Dear Anonymous,

There seems to be a penchant for demanding perfection of our leaders while allowing ample latitude for our own behavior. Let me see if I can clarify the situation.

1) There are no perfect leaders–or followers. The Savior is the only sinless person.

2) Leaders are called by inspiration of the Lord from among the pool of people He has to work with.

3) The Lord honors and respects the authority that He has delegated to those who hold keys of the priesthood.

4) Those who hold the keys, *i.e.*, who may call others to positions of responsibility, are responsible to Lord for the choices they make and for their own deportment while in office.

5) If those in office commit gross improprieties, they will be removed from office by the proper authorities. Until they are removed from office their administration will be honored and accepted.

Let me give you one small example. The father of an eight-year-old child has committed a sin for which he will eventually be excommunicated. At the time of the child's baptism, however, his sin is unknown to the authorities and he is authorized by his bishop to baptize his child. After the baptism, the sin comes to light and the father is excommunicated. Does the child have to be rebaptized? No! The father, at the time, held the requisite authority and the ordinance is recognized by our Heavenly Father. Will the father be held accountable for his actions in sinning in the first place, in not confessing when he should have, in performing a priesthood ordinance knowing that he was unworthy to do so? Absolutely!!

6) If a priesthood authority who has committed a gross sin goes to the temple before the sin has become known and performs a vicarious ordinance, will that ordinance be valid? Yes!

7) Will the temple be desecrated by his presence? If it is, it will be desecrated in commensurate degree by every person who enters, because no one who enters the temple is without sin.

8) When we raise our hands to sustain our leaders, that act is the sign of a covenant that we make with the Lord that we will SUSTAIN them so long as they are in office. We are commanded not to judge others.

Judge not, that ye be not judged. For with what judgment ye judge, ye shall be judged: and with what measure ye mete, it shall be measured to you again." (Matthew 7:1-2)

If we demand our pound of flesh, requiring that others always act above reproach, we have condemned ourselves to the same harsh judgement that we impose on others. How much better would it be if we all had forgiving hearts and tried to help and uplift those who are struggling, rather than censuring them for inappropriate behavior. The observance of inappropriate behavior should be a signal for our help rather than a signal for our condemnation. Someone said, "Forgiveness is the fragrance that the violet sheds on the heal that has crushed it."

—Gramps

What should I do to become a member of the Church of Jesus Christ of Latter-day Saints?

Gramps,

I'm considering conversion, and I am curious as to the process that I would have to follow. What I am asking for is a description of the process and an explanation. Thank you.

Anonymous, from Michigan

P.S. I'm currently Roman Catholic.

Dear Anonymous,

If you were to decide to become a member of the Church of Jesus Christ of Latter-day Saints you would be one of about 300,000 people each year that are doing so. The procedure is quite simple. You could contact the church in your area and ask the missionaries to give you the missionary lessons. You could find them by visiting a local unit of the church (These are called Wards and are the equivalent of the Catholic Parish), or you could call the missionaries on the phone. The number could be found in the directory listing for the Church of Jesus Christ of Latter-day Saints, under Mission, if there is a local mission in your area. Or the Internet address is: www.lds.org.

The missionaries will be happy to come to your home and present six formal lessons that are designed to acquaint you with the basic doctrine and procedures of the church. They will introduce you to the Book of Mormon, which is a companion scripture to the Bible, and they will invite you to ask God, our Heavenly Father, for guidance in the decision that you make as to whether or not to join the church. Usually, before the end of the lessons, those who are sincerely interested in seeking the truth receive a feeling from the Lord that indeed the Church of Jesus Christ of Latter-day Saints is God's kingdom on the earth and they request entrance into the church by baptism.

Baptism into the church is performed by a person authorized by the holy priesthood to do so. The missionaries are so authorized, as are most of the adults and young men over age sixteen. (As with the

Catholics, priesthood in the LDS Church is restricted to male members). Baptism is performed by immersion, that is, the candidate is submersed under the water. There are baptismal fonts in many of the LDS Chapels, and appropriate white clothing is provided for the baptismal candidates.

Following your baptism, you will be confirmed a member of the church by the laying on of hands, again administered by the holy priesthood. You then will be a full-fledged member of the church and will join in the fellowship of the Saints, as the church members are called.

—Gramps,

WHO WAS PELEG?

Gramps,
Please tell me what you know about this person called Peleg. Was
he a Priesthood holder? Why was the earth changed so violently.? We
know so little about this person.
JLeo

Dear JLeo,
The only source information on Peleg is found in Genesis 10:25 and 11:16-19, as quoted below:

> *And unto Eber were born two sons: the name of one was Peleg;*
> *for in his days was the earth divided; and his brother's name was*
> *Joktan. (Genesis 10:25)*
> *And Eber lived four and thirty years, and begat Peleg: And Eber*
> *lived after he begat Peleg four hundred and thirty years, and begat*
> *sons and daughters. And Peleg lived thirty years, and begat Reu: And*
> *Peleg lived after he begat Reu two hundred and nine years, and begat*
> *sons and daughters. (Genesis 11:16-19)*

However, from that information it has been deduced that Peleg was born in 2247 B.C., 101 years after the flood, and that he lived to be 239 years old.

President John Taylor made these interesting comments about Peleg and the violent changes in the earth's topology:

"How far the flood may have contributed to produce the various changes, as to the division of the earth into broken fragments, island and continents, mountains and valleys, we have not been informed; the change must have been considerable. But after the flood, in the days of Peleg, the earth was divided— See Gen. 10:25,—a short history, to be sure, of so great an event; but still it will account for the mighty revolution which rolled the sea from its own place in the north, and brought it to interpose between different portions of the earth, which were thus parted asunder, and moved into something near their present form; this, together with the earthquakes, revolutions, and commotions which have since taken place, have all contributed to reduce the face of the earth to its present state; while the great curses which have fallen upon different portions, because of the wickedness of men, will account for the stagnant swamps, the sunken lakes, the dead seas, and great deserts." (*The Government of God*, Ch.12)

—Gramps

How can I gain enough courage to Bear my Testimony?

Gramps:
How do you get the courage to bear your testimony? I am so scared to stand in front of people and talk. I haven't done it for many years and now I have a small son and I want him to know that I have a testimony, and I also want him to be able to bear his one day. But right now I am not a very good example.
Connie, from Utah

Dear Connie,
I know exactly how you feel! When I was young, I was absolutely petrified to speak in public. I have died a thousand deaths behind the pulpit. However, I have learned the following: we are frightened with the unfamiliar and feel comfortable with that which is familiar to us. The only way I know of to get over the fear of talking in front of people it to talk in front of people.

There is no doubt that you can muster the courage one time to bear your testimony. It may not be a pleasant experience. In fact, it could be quite embarrassing. However, if you let that embarrassment deter you from trying again, you're lost. You might make a resolution to bear a brief testimony each month at fast meeting. You might plan to always be the second one to get up. If you were to do that, within a year you would feel quite comfortable at the pulpit and would be the example you would like to be for your son. You may even invite him to come with you on occasion and help him through is testimony.

—Gramps

HOW CAN I OVERCOME SOME OF MY STRONG PAST BELIEFS AS I CONSIDER MEMBERSHIP IN THE CHURCH OF JESUS CHRIST OF LATTER-DAY SAINTS?

Dear Gramps,

My question deals with doctrine. I am currently a protestant, but I came from a Catholic upbringing. My current set of beliefs is probably 90% from studying scripture and maybe 10% from church affiliation. Above anything, I want to know God in all of His fullness, and in doing so I am reading the Book of Mormon with an open mind and praying in faith for God to show me "if these things are true." I can see myself accepting the Book of Mormon as true and even in accepting Joseph Smith as a prophet. My problem comes with these new doctrines and beliefs that are nowhere near what I have believed and often times just the opposite. How would you suggest this being handled?

BD

Dear BD,

Congratulations! You have espoused one of the noblest desires that can be encompassed by mankind. John has told us that

this is life eternal, that they might know thee the only true God, and Jesus Christ, whom thou hast sent. (John 17:3)

God is our Father:
> *Furthermore we have had fathers of our flesh which corrected us, and we gave them reverence: shall we not much rather be in subjection unto the Father of spirits, and live?* (Hebrews 12:9),

and he loves His children:
> *As the Father hath loved me, so have I loved you: continue ye in my love.* (John 15:9)

Since our loving Father desires that we come to know him, who He is, and what great things He has done to provide for the salvation of His children, He will help us to come to know him.

It is appropriate that we learn what we can about God from the revelations that He has given to his prophets. So, it is important to study the scriptures, as you have done, wherein the knowledge of God is revealed to man. However, the scriptures can lend themselves to various interpretations and there are many different notions about who God is and what He is like. Obviously, there can only be one truth.

There is one sure way to find the true interpretation of the scriptures and that is to ask God the Father, in the name of Jesus Christ, if He will reveal the truthfulness of the scriptures to you. Of course, in the asking, we must do all within our power to live in compliance with what we understand to be His will. The great and last prophet of the Nephite nation, Moroni, put it this way:

> *And when ye shall receive these things, I would exhort you that ye would ask God, the Eternal Father, in the name of Christ, if these things are not true; and if ye shall ask with a sincere heart, with real intent, having faith in Christ, he will manifest the truth of it unto you, by the power of the Holy Ghost. And by the power of the Holy Ghost ye may know the truth of all things.* (Moroni 10:4-5)

Perhaps it would be well to hold in question all your former beliefs in anticipation of receiving an answer to your prayers. If, for instance, you were to ask the Lord to reveal to you that the Book of Mormon is indeed the word of God and contains, as it claims, the fullness of the everlasting gospel, and if the Lord were to answer your prayer and give to you a firm, unalterable conviction that the book were true, then all your doctrinal questions would be solved.

—Gramps

IS THERE SOME PROOF THAT THE WINE THE SAVIOR DRANK WAS NON-FERMENTED?

Dear Gramps,
I have some coworkers who would like me to prove that the wine Jesus drank at the last supper was non-alcoholic grape juice. They say that they want to see it in writing by some "scholar" that is not a member of the LDS faith.
Kris, from Utah

Dear Kris,

Do you think that your coworkers would be convinced if some non-LDS scholars were to agree with LDS scholars? The only information available is that which is written in the scriptures. But there is some understanding among many scholars as to what was meant by the various types of wine mentioned in the scriptures.

I'm sorry that I can't cite any non-LDS scholars on this subject. If your coworkers, who are non-LDS, had any real interest in the answer, perhaps they could look up their own sources. Rather than responding to such a devious challenge, who don't you ask them to "prove" that any wine that the Savior drank *was* alcoholic?

Here's one statement by LDS scholars on the subject. (I think that any unbiased person would recognize that this information is as objective as any that your friends could find).

"The use of 'pure wine' in the Sacrament is permitted. But what is 'pure wine' if not the pure juice of the grape, before it has been adulterated by the process of fermentation? No fewer than thirteen Hebrew and Greek terms are rendered in our Bible by the word 'wine.' There is the pure grape juice, and a kind of grape syrup, the thickness of which made it necessary to mingle water with it previously to drinking. (Prov. 9:2, 5) There was a wine made strong and inebriating by the addition of drugs, such as myrrh, mandragora, and opiates. (Prov. 23:30; Isa. 5:22) Of the pure wine which was diluted with water, or milk, Wisdom invites her friends to drink freely. (Prov. 9:2, 5) There was also 'wine on the lees,' which is supposed to have been 'preserves' or 'jellies.' (Isa. 25:6) The 'pure wine' is not an intoxicating, but a harmless liquid." (Smith and Sjodahl, in *Doctrine and Covenants Commentary*, Sec. 89, p. 572)

—Gramps

WHAT HAPPENED TO THE ARTIFACTS IN THE TEMPLE WHEN THE SAINTS WERE FORCED TO LEAVE NAUVOO?

Dear gramps,
I am wondering how the temple property and artifacts were han-
dled and disposed of when the church left Nauvoo?
9875

Dear 9875,
I believe that the church made no formal disposition of the materials and artifacts that were in the Nauvoo Temple. You will remember that they were forced by armed mobs to flee from their homes while the temple was being cannonaded. James E. Talmage, in his *Articles of Faith*, p.155, stated that

> "The Temple at Nauvoo was destroyed through malicious incendiarism."

So I imagine that it was probably looted by the mob and then burned.

President Joseph F. Smith was a boy of about six years old when the exodus came. Here is an excerpt from his account of the event—

> "I can remember the time when I was quite a little boy, when we were hurried very unceremoniously across the river Mississippi from the city of Nauvoo just previous to the bombardment of the town by the mob. I had a great anxiety then—that is for a child—to know where on earth we were going to. I knew we had left home. We had left it willingly—because we were obliged to—we left it in a hurry, and we were not far away when we heard the cannonade on the other side of the river." (*Journal of Discourses*, Vol.24, p.150, Joseph F. Smith, December 3, 1882)

—Gramps

WHY HAVE NOT MY PRAYERS BEEN ANSWERED?

Dear Gramps,
My family has been struggling with financial problems for a while,
due to my Dad's being unemployed. I have fasted and prayed many days
and nights along with the rest of my family and nothing has happened
for almost a year. Why isn't the Lord answering my prayers?
Sarah

Dear Sarah,

It is natural for us to request the Lord to solve all our problems, and it is also appropriate that we pour out our hearts to Him seeking His intervention. However, the fact that our prayers are not answered according our own time frame does not mean that they have not been heard, nor that in the appropriate time of the Lord they won't be answered.

On the last day of November of 1838, Joseph Smith had been court marshaled and condemned to be shot the following morning. General Alexander W. Doniphan refused to carry out the order saying that it was cold-blooded murder. His refusal frightened the general in command of the mob that was, at that time, expelling the saints from the state of Missouri. The whole church prayed for the Prophet's release from Liberty Jail. Five months later, on March 20, while still in prison, the Prophet poured out his soul to the Lord, pleading for relief. You can read his prayer in the first part of D&C 121. The Lord answered his prayer, but did not immediately release him from prison; rather, the Lord gave Joseph some very sage advise—

My son, peace be unto thy soul; thine adversity and thine afflictions shall be but a small moment; And then, if thou endure it well, God shall exalt thee on high; thou shalt triumph over all thy foes. Thy friends do stand by thee, and they shall hail thee again with warm hearts and friendly hands. Thou art not yet as Job; thy friends do not contend against thee, neither charge thee with transgression, as they did Job. And they who do charge thee with transgression, their hope shall be blasted, and their prospects shall melt away as the hoar frost melteth before the burning rays of the rising sun. (D&C 121:8-11)

And from that extremely difficult experience came some of the most marvelous and profound revelations of the Restoration.

The Prophet made two unsuccessful attempts to escape before he was finally released. Was the Lord indifferent to his pleas, or was Joseph being trained and schooled by the things that he was required to suffer? The road through mortality was not designed as an easy path but as a proving ground where we will be confronted with opposition and where our faith will be tested. But the Lord has given us this promise

> Therefore, he giveth this promise unto you, with an immutable covenant that they shall be fulfilled; and all things wherewith you have been afflicted shall work together for your good, and to my name's glory, saith the Lord. (D&C 98:3)

So don't feel that the Lord has not heard your prayers nor that He will not answer them in such a way that the deprivations that you now are suffering will be converted into blessings for you and your family. We must have faith, patience, and have full confidence that the Lord will do His work in His own way. If, on the other hand, we lose faith, we may forfeit the blessings that otherwise would be ours.

—Gramps

WHAT EVER HAPPENED TO THE GOLDEN PLATES FROM WHICH THE BOOK OF MORMON WAS TRANSLATED?

Gramps,
Where can I find out what happened to the golden plates when Joseph Smith finished the translation of the Book of Mormon? Is there anything that directly states what happened to them? Thank you,
Jack, from California

Dear Jack,
The golden plates upon which the Book of Mormon was written have had quite a history, and it is rather well documented. We first learn about them from the visit of the Angel Moroni to Joseph Smith on

September 21, 1823. During this visit Moroni told Joseph that the plates and the Urim and Thummim were buried nearby, and Moroni showed Joseph the plates' location. The next day Joseph went to the place, removed a stone that covered the receptacle where they were, and saw both the plates and the Urim and Thummim, just as Moroni had said. The plates were retrieved by the Prophet four years later on September 22, 1827.

When the translation was finished the Prophet returned the plates to the Angel Moroni, but the exact date is apparently unknown. We read in the Encyclopedia of Mormonism that the plates were returned to the Angel Moroni in 1829, which would have to have been after they were shown to the Three Witnesses in June of that year. Elder Bruce R. McConkie makes the following statement in *Mormon Doctrine*, p.327,

"The actual translation of the portion we now have as the Book of Mormon did not take place until between April 7 and June 11, 1829. Thereafter the plates were returned to the custody of Moroni. *(Jos. Smith 2:27-65)*"

—Gramps

WHAT HAS HAPPENED TO THE DESCENDANTS OF BRIGHAM YOUNG?

Dear Gramps,
What has happened to the descendants of Brigham Young? There must be many of them by now. However, we do not hear very much about them in church circles these days. Thank You,
L.L.

Dear LL,
Without a doubt the descendants of Brigham Young are extremely numerous. However, citing one's genealogy for public examination is not a common practice. We may hear a good deal from his descendants in church, but not be aware that they are his descendants. In a prayer by

Elder Orson Pratt on the occasion of the dedication of the Logan Temple, he prayed:

"O Lord, bless him whom thou hast inspired, even thy servant, President Brigham Young...Bless, O Lord, his generations after him, that they may rise up and be mighty men in the earth; that they may be clothed with the power and the spirit, so abundantly manifested upon their respected father; and may his descendants, in all generations, enjoy, even more abundantly, superior wisdom and knowledge and understanding from the heavens, to discern in their several callings all things which shall tend to the blessing and glory and future exaltation and progress of mankind on the earth; and that there never may be a time or period, in all the generations of this world, when he shall not be represented by a numerous posterity, who shall enjoy the fullness of the holy Priesthood, and the powers, blessings, and keys thereof." *(Journal of Discourses,* Vol.19, p.33)

—Gramps

IS IT OKAY TO JOIN A SUPPORT GROUP THAT MEETS ON SUNDAY?

Hi Gramps,

Is it okay to join a support group for therapy that only meets on Sundays? It is the only support group in my area and I really think that I would benefit from by going to. I just don't want to break the Sabbath. Of course, I will discuss this with my bishop, but your opinion would be great.

Anon.

Dear Anon,

There are so many kinds of support groups with so many different agendas that it would be impossible to comment on your question in any meaningful way. Unless there is a specific health-related problem, support groups are generally discouraged be the church. However, you are right in appealing to your bishop. I could give you no better advise than to approach him and to listen to his council.

—Gramps

WHAT DOES IT MEAN TO BE FROM THE TRIBE OF BENJAMIN?

Dear Gramps,

This is in reference to the tribes of Israel. Most members of the church seem to be from either Ephraim or Manasseh. In my patriarchal blessing I was told I was from the tribe of Benjamin. That wasn't one of the ten lost tribes was it? What does it mean?

Lori, Oklahoma

Dear Lori,

The kingdom of Israel was divided about 975 B.C. Ten of the tribes revolted and followed Jeroboam as their king and became known as the Kingdom of Israel or the Kingdom of Ephraim. Judah and part of the tribe of Benjamin maintained their allegiance to their monarch and following Rehoboam, the son of Solomon. They became known as the Kingdom of Judah.

Now, concerning your own lineage, President Joseph Fielding Smith had this to say:

"When a man who is of Israel joins the church, his tribal relationship does not change. For instance, a descendant of Judah would be classed as of the tribe of Judah, a descendant of Benjamin as of the tribe of Benjamin, and so with those of other tribes." (*Doctrines of Salvation*, Vol.3, p.247)

So you are not descended from any of the lost ten tribes (most of the members of the church today seem to be of the tribe of Ephraim), but are descended from those who remained at Jerusalem when the tribes were divided. You may know that Paul was of the tribe of Benjamin. In writing his epistle to the Roman saints he said:

For I also am an Israelite, of the seed of Abraham, of the tribe of Benjamin. (Romans 11:1)

—Gramps

WHY DO THEY CALL CHARLIE HORSES, CHARLIE HORSES?

Gramps,
I want to ask you a question. Seriously! I'll be expecting a real answer. Here's my question: Why do they call charlie-horses, charlie-horses?
Jason

Dear Jason,

In the first place "charlie horse" is spelled "charley horse." Charley horse is an American expression of uncertain origin. It dates from the 1880s and may have been originally baseball slang. It refers to a painful involuntary cramp in an arm or leg muscle, usually that of an athlete, as a result of a muscular strain or a blow. There are lots of theories about its origin. There's a persistent story that the original Charley was a lame horse of that name that pulled the roller at the White Sox ballpark in Chicago near the end of last century. The American Dialect Society's archives reproduced a story that was printed in the *Washington Post* in 1907, long enough after the event that people were trying to explain something already mysterious. This piece said it referred to the pitcher Charley Radbourne, nicknamed Old Hoss, who suffered this problem during a game in the 1880s; the condition was then named by putting together his first name and the second half of his nickname. The first recorded use, again from the ADS archives, is from *Sporting Life* of 1886; that and other citations suggest it was coined not long before.

–Gramps

HOW SHOULD I TREAT MY NON-LDS FAMILY WHO OPPOSE MY FORTHCOMING TEMPLE MARRIAGE?

Dear Gramps,

I am planning on getting married in the temple within the next year after my intended graduates trade school. I am so excited and can't wait!! My problem is, none of my family are members and aren't very accepting of the fact I am "LDS." They've made comments, without me telling them anything, that "they had better be able to attend my wedding ceremony, or else," and that they don't want people from my church there. How can I break it to them that they cant be at the actual ceremony? I've been trying, but it's so hard. Also, my boyfriend's mother seems not to like the idea too much. She feels we should wait until his second brother is home from his mission. She asked if we've prayed about it. Of course we have and we've both received revelation on this matter. Could this just be Satan sinking the teeth of opposition where it hurts, or should we go with the Spirit? (PS: we're 23 and 24 years old)

C. Smith

Dear C. Smith,

I can appreciate some of the difficulties you face contemplating a temple marriage as the only member of the church in your family. All the difficulties that you mention may not be resolvable prior to your marriage. However, I'm sure that you will do what you can to explain your circumstance to your family. Perhaps you may want to get them all together to announce your wedding plans, and explain to them the sacredness of the covenants you will be making with one another, and that such covenants are available only within the sacred precincts of the holy temple.

You might tell them that the purpose of a reception would be to greet family and friends and rejoice together in celebration of the sacred event, and that you hope that they will share your joy at that occasion.

If they choose to oppose such a plan, then you have a choice to make—either to enter into the holy covenant of eternal marriage with its limitless blessings, or to have a civil marriage in order to placate your family. I would suggest that you might do much more good to your family by demonstrating to them the depth of your commitment to sacred things than by trying to satisfy their desires by denying the infinite blessings of eternity associated with the eternal marriage covenant.

If you do what you know is right, and yet show sympathy and love toward those who may oppose your actions, you will undoubtedly stand as an exemplar of sacred principles. Your family will without doubt soften their hearts toward you and your husband as you continue to demonstrate love and acceptance of them, especially in the face of their opposition to your plans.

—Gramps

WHY WERE MEMBERS OF THE BLACK RACE RESTRICTED FROM HOLDING THE PRIESTHOOD UNTIL 1978?

Gramps,
I'm a new convert to the church as of a year ago. How do I explain the Lord's not allowing blacks to hold the priesthood until 1978? I have a strong testimony of the church, but it's hard to explain to my family, who are born-again Christians. What do I say, Gramps, in your opinion?

Josh, from California

Dear Josh,
The Lord withheld the priesthood from the descendants of Cain from the very beginning. The descendants of Cain were cursed by having the priesthood withheld from them, but they were blessed by being given a black skin to protect them from others with evil intent.

> *And the Lord said unto him, Therefore whosoever slayeth Cain, vengeance shall be taken on him sevenfold. And the Lord set a mark upon Cain, lest any finding him should kill him.* (Genesis 4:15)

The withholding of the priesthood from the descendants of Cain is recorded in the Book of Abraham.

> *Now this king of Egypt was a descendant from the loins of Ham, and was a partaker of the blood of the Canaanites by birth. From this descent sprang all the Egyptians, and thus the blood of the Canaanites was preserved in the land...Pharaoh, being a righteous man, established his kingdom and judged his people wisely and justly all his days, seeking earnestly to imitate that order established by the fathers in the first generations, in the days of the first patriarchal reign, even in the reign of Adam, and also of Noah, his father, who blessed him with the blessings of the earth, and with the blessings of wisdom, but cursed him as pertaining to the Priesthood.* (Abraham 1:21-26)

Although the Lord withheld the priesthood from the black race since the days of Cain, every president of the church, from the time of Joseph Smith, prophesied that the day would come when those of the black race would be permitted to hold the priesthood. Elder Milton R. Hunter recorded the following:

> "Brigham Young did not originate the doctrine that Negroes could not hold the Priesthood in this life but some day some of them may be granted that privilege, but he was taught it by the Prophet Joseph." (Milton R. Hunter, *Pearl of Great Price Commentary,* p.142)

And from the history of Wilford Woodruff—

> "Any man having one drop of the seed of Cain in him cannot receive the Priesthood; but the day will come when all that race will be redeemed and possess all the blessings which we now have." (*History of Wilford Woodruff,* p. 351)

And Elder Bruce R. McConkie has written the following—

> "'Sing and rejoice, O daughter of Zion: for, lo, I come, and I will dwell in the midst of thee, saith the Lord. The Lord Jesus Christ shall reign personally upon the earth. And many nations shall be joined to the Lord in that day, and shall be my people.' Gentile nations shall be converted; the blacks shall receive the priesthood; nations long outside the pale of saving grace shall come into the fold and shall rise up and bless Abraham as their father." (Bruce R. McConkie, *The Millennial Messiah,* p.599)

It is important to note that it was the Lord, not man, that withheld the priesthood from the blacks. Thus it could not be restored to them except by the word of the Lord. That marvelous day came in June 1978 when President Spencer W. Kimball received a revelation from the Lord extending the blessings of the priesthood to all worthy male members of the church.

> *The long-promised day has come when every faithful, worthy man in the church may receive the holy priesthood, with power to exercise its divine authority, and enjoy with his loved ones every blessing that flows therefrom, including the blessings of the temple. Accordingly, all worthy male members of the church may be ordained to the priesthood without regard for race or color. (Doctrine and Covenants, Official Declaration—2)*

—Gramps

WILL I JUST BE KNITTING SOCKS DURING THE MILLENNIUM?

Dear Gramps,

I'm single and will likely never marry. I've heard that if worthy sisters do not have a chance to marry while on earth, they will have that blessing in the Millennium. I always thought I would be kneeling at the altar with someone, but it hasn't happened. Now, I understand that mortals may be doing that work for me, and, to be honest, I really don't like that idea at all. I looked forward to that event since I was a child. It's sad enough that I never had the chance. But to still not be able to kneel at the altar with a worthy husband is pretty disappointing! Another question: if we single people, when resurrected, are not able to do temple work, what are we to do for a thousand years, knit socks?!

Winnifred, from Europe

Dear Winnifred,
Let me quote from President Joseph Fielding Smith.

"Will resurrected beings during the millennium actually take part in the endowment work of the temple along with mortal beings? The answer to this question is no! That is, they will not assist in performing the ordinances. Resurrected beings will assist in furnishing information which is not otherwise available, but mortals will have to do the ordinance work in the temples. Baptism, confirmation, ordination, endowment, and sealings all pertain to this mortal life and are ordinances required of those who are in mortality. Provision has been made for these ordinances to be performed vicariously for those who are worthy but who died without the opportunity in this life of receiving these ordinances in person." *(Doctrines of Salvation,* Vol.2, p.178)

Now about knitting socks: The sealing of husband to wife in the temple takes about five minutes. There will very possibly be many more resurrected beings than mortals living on the earth during the Millennium, and I imagine that there will be plenty to do to keep them all busy doing the work of the Lord. We know very little about the particular activities and assignments that resurrected people will have during the Millennium, but surely one of them will be, as President Smith said above, to help identify and gather the records of all the people who didn't have the opportunity to receive the gospel on the earth but who received it afterwards so that

> *they might be judged according to men in the flesh, but live according to God in the spirit.* (D&C 138:10)

—Gramps

WHERE CAN I GET A GOOD KILT CHEAP?

Dear Gramps,
I want to wear a kilt in the Harkness clan tartan for my wedding reception. Where can I find one for less than $300?
Sam

Dear Sam,
You might try Deseret Industries in Scotland.
—Gramps

WHAT WAS THE STATE OF RIGHTEOUSNESS OF THE DESCENDANTS OF CAIN IN THE PRE-MORTAL WORLD?

Gramps,
I have heard many conflicting stories but have yet to receive any documentation on the subject of the state of righteousness of the descendants of Cain while in the Pre-existence. I am of mixed race (black/white) and my wife is black. My children, I'm sure, will ask the same question to me and I want to give them an honest answer. Can you help?
Rowland, from Michigan

Dear Rowland,
I am not acquainted with any scripture or the writing of any of the Brethren that makes a judgment on the degree of righteous of the pre-mortal spirits of the descendants of Cain. We do know that the descendants of Cain, whatever their condition in the pre-mortal spirit world, were denied the priesthood down through the ages until the great revelation given to President Spencer W. Kimball that has now become part of our scripture.

Incidentally, the curse that was inherited by the descendants of Cain was not a black skin, but their being denied the priesthood. The black skin that they were given was actually a blessing. It was given to protect them against those that would try to take revenge on them for the sin of their progenitor.

> *And the LORD said unto him, Therefore whosoever slayeth Cain, vengeance shall be taken on him sevenfold. And the LORD set a mark upon Cain, lest any finding him should kill him.* (Genesis 4:15)

—Gramps

DURING THE CIVIL WAR DID THE MAJORITY OF THE SAINTS LEAN TOWARD THE UNION OR THE CONFEDERACY?

Gramps,
During the Civil War did the majority of the Saints lean toward the Union or the Confederacy?
David

Dear David,

The slavery issue in the emerging states during the early days of the church was one of the fomenting factors for persecution against the Saints. Prior to the admission of Missouri as a state, there were an equal number of free and slave states. As Missouri applied for Statehood in 1818, numbers of people from the South emigrated to Missouri with the intent of making it a slave state. Missouri was granted statehood on August 10, 1821.

On August 13, 1831, the Prophet Joseph Smith received a revelation directing the Saints to gather together in the land of Missouri. (D&C 62) Most of the converts to the church, who were gathering to Zion at this time, were from the northern states or from England, and both groups were opposed to slavery. This influx of people, who were opposed to slavery, alarmed the Missourians and that became the focal point of much conflict.

By the time of the Civil War, the church had emigrated to the mountains of the West, where they were quite isolated from the conflict. However, the sympathies of the members were generally opposed to slavery.

—Gramps

IS IT TRUE THAT ANY ONE WHO CHOOSES NOT TO HAVE CHILDREN WILL NOT INHERIT THE CELESTIAL KINGDOM?

Gramps,
I have been told by a "well meaning" neighbor that anyone who chooses to not have children will not reach the Celestial Kingdom. Is this true?
Marge, from Utah

Dear Marge,
Let's see if we can identify some of those who will inherit the Celestial Kingdom. First, in the Priesthood manual for 2000, *Teachings of Presidents of the Church: Joseph F. Smith*, it would be interesting to look at chapter 15, entitled "The Salvation of Little Children." Here we learn that "little children who die before they reach the years of accountability are redeemed by the blood of Christ," and inherit the Celestial Kingdom.

"Such children are in the bosom of the Father. They will inherit their glory and their exaltation, and they will not be deprived of the blessings that belong to them, . . and in the wisdom and mercy and economy of God our Heavenly Father, all that could have been obtained and enjoyed by these if they had been permitted to live in the flesh will be provided for them hereafter." (*Collected Discourses,* Vol. 4, Funeral Services for Daniel Wells Grant, March 12, 1895)

We read in the Doctrine and Covenants that not only will little children inherit the Celestial Kingdom, but also that all who have died without a knowledge of this gospel, who would have received it if they had been permitted to tarry, shall be heirs of the celestial kingdom of God.

Thus came the voice of the Lord unto me, saying: All who have died without a knowledge of this gospel, who would have received it if they had been permitted to tarry, shall be heirs of the celestial kingdom of God; Also all that shall die henceforth without a knowledge of it, who would have received it with all their hearts, shall be heirs of that kingdom; For I, the Lord, will judge all men according to their works, according to the desire of their hearts. And I also beheld that all children who die before they arrive at the years of accountability are saved in the celestial kingdom of heaven. (D&C 137:7-10)

We understand also that all those who are baptized into the Lord's church, who live in accordance with their baptismal covenant, and who remain true and faithful all the days of their lives, but who are not sealed in the holy temple, although denied exaltation, will also inherit the glory of the Celestial Kingdom.

> *For these angels did not abide my law; therefore, they cannot be enlarged, but remain separately and singly, without exaltation, in their saved condition, to all eternity; and from henceforth are not gods, but are angels of God forever and ever.* (D&C 132:17)

So, it seems that your neighbor was more well meaning than well informed.

—Gramps

CAN I EXPECT THAT MY WAYWARD CHILDREN WILL REPENT AND RETURN TO THE LORD?

Dear Gramps,

I have four adult children but only one is living the gospel of Jesus Christ. They were all taught the gospel from their birth. I have been in great despair over this. I have been told that if I keep my temple covenants and strive to keep the commandments as best I can that my children will return to the "fold." Is this true and how can that be? I have an aunt who is very old and has not been in the church for fifty years and her parents, my grandparents, were true blue to their temple covenants. They have passed on now and have not been granted those blessings. I suffer great anguish over my disobedient children.

Judith, from Canada

Dear Judith,

Yours is not an uncommon lament. How many parents anguish over their disobedient children! Yet that anguish, although proper and justified for the circumstance of the moment, may be ameliorated by confidence in the blessings promised by the Lord in his holy temples. Where mercy does not apply, justice cannot be denied, and those who do wrong and remain unrepentant will pay the full price for their sins as if there had been no redemption wrought. But having paid the price, the promises made to their faithful parents in the holy temples will be honored by a just God, who is our kind and loving Father.

Our task as parents is to never lose faith or to be without hope. There is always the chance for repentance. And whether a person comes to the Lord early or late, even to the point of changing his life in the post-mortal spirit world, forgiveness and acceptance are yet available. The Lord said through Isaiah,

> *Though your sins be as scarlet, they shall be as white as snow; though they be red like crimson, they shall be as wool.* (Isaiah 1:18)

Here is what the Prophet Joseph Smith and President Joseph Fielding Smith had to say on the subject:

"The Prophet Joseph Smith declared—and he never taught a more comforting doctrine—that the eternal sealings of faithful parents and the divine promises made to them for valiant service in the Cause of Truth, would save not only themselves, but likewise their posterity. Though some of the sheep may wander, the eye of the Shepherd is upon them, and sooner or later they will feel the tentacles of Divine Providence reaching out after them and drawing them back to the fold. Either in this life or the life to come, they will return. They will have to pay their debt to justice; they will suffer for their sins; and may tread a thorny path; but if it leads them at last, like the penitent Prodigal, to a loving and forgiving father's heart and home, the painful experience will not have been in vain. Pray for your careless and disobedient children; hold on to them with your faith. Hope on, trust on, till you see the salvation of God." (Orson F. Whitney, *Conference Report*, April 1929, p.110)

"Let the father and mother, who are members of this Church and Kingdom, take a righteous course, and strive with all their might never to do a wrong, but to do good all their lives; if they have one child or one hundred children, if they conduct themselves towards them as they should, binding them to the Lord by their faith and prayers, I care not where those children go, they are bound up to their parents by an everlasting tie, and no power of earth or hell can separate them from their parents in eternity; they will return again to the fountain from whence they sprang." (Joseph Fielding Smith, *Doctrines of Salvation*)

So it remains for us to be hopeful, faithful, prayerful, kind, loving and confident.
—Gramps

WHERE DO DOGS GO WHEN THEY DIE?

Gramps,
We would like to know were dogs go when they die. We had a dog that died and she was like family. We would like to know if we will be with her in the next life. Is there a special place where they go or will she be with us?
John and Teresa

Dear John and Teresa,
In the first place, we know that all things were created spiritually before they were created temporally. In Moses 3:7 we read,
> And I, the Lord God, formed man from the dust of the ground, and breathed into his nostrils the breath of life; and man became a living soul, the first flesh upon the earth, the first man also; <u>nevertheless, all things were before created; but spiritually were they created and made according to my word</u>.

We also know that through the infinite atonement of the Savior all living things will be resurrected, the spirit reunited with the body, and will participate in eternal life. In *Answers to Gospel Question*, by Joseph Fielding Smith, we read the following:
> "Question: Do animals have spirits? If so, will they obtain the resurrection, and if so, where will they go?
> "Answer: The simple answer is that animals do have spirits and that through the redemption made by our Savior they will come forth in the resurrection to enjoy the blessing of immortal life."

Will the animals that we knew in mortality be with us in the eternity? Again, Joseph Fielding Smith has provided a definitive answer:

"It would be a very strange world where animals were not found. If, after the resurrection of the dead, we discovered that man was the only living creature with immortality, we would certainly consider it a very strange world." (*Doctrines of Salvation*, Vol.1, p.63)

"So we see that the Lord intends to save not only the earth and the heavens, not only man who dwells upon the earth, but all things which he has created. The animals, the fishes of the sea, the fowls of the air, as well as man, are to be recreated, or renewed, through the resurrection, for they too are living souls." (*Doctrines of Salvation*. Vol.1, p.74)

Since we will live on the earth during the Millennium, and if we are worthy to be on the sanctified and celestialized earth in the eternities, we would imagine that the good things of the earth, both plants and animals, will continue to be a part of it so that we would continue to enjoy their company and they ours.

—Gramps

HOW CAN I TREAT MY FRIEND'S INTEREST IN DISCUSSING THE DIFFERENCE BETWEEN HIS CHURCH AND OURS?

Dear Gramps,

How would you respond to this feedback that I receive from a good friend who is "Christian."

"I would be interested in discussing Mormonism with you. Christianity and Mormonism are exclusive, in that each claims there is only one way to God. Consequently, each doctrine teaches that all other religions are wrong. I'm convinced the truth can be determined beyond a reasonable doubt by evidence not feelings. Feelings can lie. I know at times I feel like I don't love my wife when we disagree. But just because I don't feel love at that moment doesn't mean I don't love her. I'm sure you get the point. Judgements, particularly regarding religion and faith, cannot be based on feelings alone. Devout people in every religion have experiences they feel confirm their beliefs. I am particularly

interested if there is any significant archaeology that supports Mormonism. Do you know of any?"
   How shall I answer, Gramps?
   Darren, from Colorado

Dear Darren,
I think that the first thing you need to do is to help your friend get over a very gross misunderstanding about "Mormonism." What does he mean— "Christianity and Mormonism?"!! You might point out to him that any meaningful discussion of the doctrines of the Church of Jesus Christ of Latter-day Saints is completely fruitless until he gets rid of that blasphemous, sectarian notion that the Church of Jesus Christ of Latter-day Saints is not "Christian." It is the most fundamentally Christian of all the churches. It's true that we do not subscribe to the nearly 2000-year-old tradition of the sectarian view of Deity.

If he believes that the truth can be established by evidence, he should spend some time studying the history of Christianity where he would find enough changes, modifications, and contradictions in doctrine and authority among the various Christian churches to make your head swim. Then he might look at the evidence, which is not just preponderant but overwhelming, that God the Father and His Son, Jesus Christ personally appeared to Joseph Smith, and that subsequent to that marvelous visitation the Savior appeared on several occasions to Joseph Smith and several of his associates.

Then have him examine the Book of Mormon. If he believes that the truth can be established by evidence, HE MUST STUDY THE EVIDENCE! There is more evidence, both internal and external to support the authenticity of the Book of Mormon than there is of any other book ever printed. The evidence is absolutely overwhelming. It fills volumes. As a matter of fact, I have written a couple myself. They are rather technical, but apparently that is what your evidence-seeking friend is after. The books are called *A New Witness For Christ* and *The Legacy of the Brass Plates of Laban.* A summary of the contents of the books can be found in the web site: www.h.clay.gorton.com.

Next let's look at his contention that "I'm convinced the truth can be determined beyond a reasonable doubt by evidences not feelings."

That's the approach people have been taking for the last 2000 years, and rather than discovering or establishing the truth, they have come to one wrong conclusion after another with such conflict between them that we have ended up with over 450 different Christian denominations in the United States alone, all somehow believing in the same Bible yet conflicting with each other. Does he think that he has some corner on the scientific method, or on the deductive or inductive processes, or some great intuitive power that he can rationalize eternal truth from the "evidence" at hand? GIVE ME A BREAK! He has already stumbled on the pebble of the error that Mormons are not Christians, and he has fallen on his face.

While it's true that the truth is not established by feelings, the evidence on which the truth is established is so powerful that it is almost always accompanied by deep feelings. Part of your friend's problem (he says he is convinced that he can determine the truth by evidence, alone) is that he is blind to any evidence for which there is an emotional attachment. GIVE ME ANOTHER BREAK!

Concerning archeological evidence to support the claims of the Book of Mormon, again the evidence is so preponderant that even a lengthy summary here could never do it justice. Suffice it to say that in the last 170 years since the publication of the Book of Mormon, although every attempt has been made by its detractors to discredit it, not one shred of evidence supports their views. On the contrary, archeological evidence in support of the Book of Mormon now fills volumes. But more than archeological evidence, such things as the language structure of the book, the terms and concepts found therein, its historical consistency, and its prophetic nature are incontrovertible evidences of its authenticity.

Perhaps a final approach to learning the truth could be mentioned to your friend. If there is a God, and if he did restore his Kingdom through the Prophet Joseph Smith, and if the church that he established is indeed the true and living church with the Savior at it's head, all your friend need do to find out those things for himself is to ask God if they are true, and if he will ask with sincere intent, having faith in Christ, the truthfulness of those things will be revealed to him by the Holy Ghost.

That will be an emotional, feeling experience, but he will be able to comprehend it because God is able to make Himself understood.

Now, if your friend wants to consider a scientific experiment, let's look at an at experimental procedure and the predicted results that are outlined in the Book of Mormon, Moroni 10:4.

Here is the procedure–

1. *And when ye shall receive these things,*

i.e., READ THE BOOK OF MORMON

2. *I would exhort you that ye would ask God, the Eternal Father, in the name of Christ, if these things are not true*;

Pray about it– a simple and direct procedure

3. *and if ye shall ask with a sincere heart, with real intent,*

This experiment has a psychological component. The prayer must be with a sincere heart and with real intent. In other words, the person must really want to know if the book is true.

4. *having faith in Christ*

Another psychological element. There must be on the part of the supplicant an abiding confidence that Jesus Christ is the Savior of the world and the Redeemer of mankind, that His Father does hear and answer prayers that are proffered in His name.

If those conditions are met, the results are:

He will manifest the truth of it unto you, by the power of the Holy Ghost.

Now, one of the tests of a scientific experiment is repeatability. There has been no scientific experiment in the history of the world that has been performed as many times as this one—all with the same positive results. Everyone who has a testimony of the Book of Mormon (over 11 million on the earth, now) has performed this experiment and has verified the results.

If your friend has any sincerity at all in what he is asking you, he will try the experiment under the published conditions. If he is not willing to try the experiment, then you may know that he is a false person and only wants to dissuade you from the truth.

—Gramps

IS TAKING MEDICINE BREAKING THE FAST?

Dear Gramps,

I understand that we should not fast when we are sick as we would be breaking the fast to take the medicine. But what do people do who always have to take medicine with food? My grandparents have prescription medicines they have had to take for years. But they still say they are fasting. True?

Lindsay

Dear Lindsay,

The Pharisees were bent on obeying the letter of the law and were condemned by Christ for it. The Savior *violated* the Jewish law on several occasions—only because the law had been fulfilled in Him. But the Pharisees were incensed and sought to put him to death.

We should obey the laws of the gospel by applying judgement and good sense. President Joseph F. Smith said

"A man may fast and pray till he kills himself, and there isn't any necessity for it; nor wisdom in it. I say to my brethren, when they are fasting, and praying for the sick, and for those who need faith and prayer, do not go beyond what is wise and prudent in fasting and prayer." (Joseph F. Smith, *Gospel Doctrine*, p.368)

If a person is required to take medication to maintain his health, it would be foolish for him to deny the medication and suffer dire consequences to adhere to the letter of the law.

Why do we fast in the first place? It seems that there are two principle reasons:

1) that by voluntarily depriving the body of food and inducing a feeling of hunger, we learn to subject the demands of the body to the dictates of the spirit. In this way, fasting gives us spiritual strength. We may then apply that strength to dominating and controlling other passions and appetites of the body.

2) by giving what we would have spent for food as a fast offering, we are helping to feed those who suffer hunger by necessity rather than by choice.

Your grandparents can easily fulfil the second purpose of fasting by contributing a generous fast offering even if they don't abstain from food for two meals. Concerning the first purpose, perhaps for them, eating the food necessary to take their medicine would require as much self discipline as would fasting.

—Gramps

WHO WAS THE VERY FIRST GOD AND HOW DID HE COME TO BE?

Gramps,
I just had to ask you the age-old question everybody's always wondered about…Who was the very first God and how did He come to be?
Kevin, from Nevada

Dear Kevin,

The idea of beginnings is indeed an age old question. We have a narrow perspective of reality while living in mortality. We have the perception that everything must have a beginning and an end. People are born and then they die. Houses are erected and are then disassembled. Activities start and end. Days come and go. We have an ingrained notion regarding the past that is no more and that the future is yet to come.

But our present perception does not reflect reality. It reminds me of the two caterpillars who were talking to one another as a butterfly flew overhead. One caterpillar said to the other, "You'll never get me up in one of those things!"

Life does continue; birth is not the beginning and death is not the end. The house was created from preexisting materials and the materials remain after the house is destroyed.

The concept of the progression of the Gods has been taught since the time of Joseph Smith. President Lorenzo Snow couched the concept in the couplet

"As man now is, our God once was; As God now is, so man may be, and thus unfolds our destiny."

The concept of eternity does not admit to beginnings and endings. There simply are no firsts. There never has been a man but who had two parents—a mother and a father. There is no end to our universe. There is no frontier to space. The idea of the start of the universe at the event of the "Big Bang" is a fiction, but it is believed by much of the scientific world because it is mathematically logical. In time that theory will give way, as so many have before it, to be replaced by other theories hopefully somewhat more consistent with the truths of eternity.

One of the hymns found in our hymn books poetically depicts the reality of eternity, as follows—

If you could hie to Kolob in the twinkling of an eye,
And then continue onward with that same speed to fly,
D'ye think that you could ever, through all eternity,
Find out the generation where Gods began to be?
Or see the grand beginning, where space did not extend?
Or view the last creation where Gods and matter end?
Methinks the Spirit whispers, "No man has found 'pure space,' "
Nor seen the outside curtains, where nothing has a place.

The works of God continue, and worlds and lives abound;
Improvement and progression have one eternal round.
There is no end to matter; there is no end to space;
There is no end to "spirit," there is no end to race.

There is no end to virtue; there is no end to might;
There is no end to wisdom; there is no end to light;
There is no end to union; there is no end to youth;
There is no end to priesthood; there is no end to truth.

There is no end to glory; there is no end to love;
There is no end to being; there is no death above;
There is no end to glory; there is no end to love;
There is no end to being; there is no death above.

—Gramps

HOW MANY TIMES WILL THE LORD FORGIVE US FOR COMMITTING THE SAME SIN?

Dear Gramps,
How many times will the Lord forgive us? Every time one truly
repents and refrains from their sin for a long time, then falls again into
the same sin? How many time will the Lord forgive for the same trans-
gression?
Creta, from Washington, D.C.

Dear Creta,
The key words in your question is "TRULY repents." The Lord will
forgive us as often as we really and truly repent.

> *Yea, and as often as my people repent will I forgive them their*
> *trespasses against me.* (Mosiah 26:30)

But what is repentance? It is explained very simply in D&C 58:
42-43:

> *Behold, he who has repented of his sins, the same is forgiven, and*
> *I, the Lord, remember them no more. By this ye may know if a man*
> *repenteth of his sins–behold, <u>he will confess them and forsake them</u>.*

One thing is confession, that's the easy part. The other is to forsake
the sin. When one forsakes a sin, that doesn't just mean he has quit
doing it. Bank robbers, for example, quit robbing when they are in jail,
but that does not mean that they have repented. Repentance means to
change. The idea of forsaking a sin is to get it out of your system so it
is no longer a part of you, no longer a habit, no longer a part of your
personality and character. Then the scripture applies–

> *he who has repented of his sins, the same is forgiven.*

Now, after repenting, if a person again succumbs to temptation and
commits again the same sin, he will be accountable for that sin and for
the ones from which he had previously repented.

> *And now, verily I say unto you, I, the Lord, will not lay any sin*
> *to your charge; go your ways and sin no more; but unto that soul*
> *who sinneth shall the former sins return, saith the Lord your God.*
> (D&C 82:7)

Then you pull yourself together and repent again, and you will find a Savior most eager to help.
—Gramps

ARE WE TO BELIEVE IN THE THEOLOGY PORTRAYED BY THE 'TOUCHED BY AN ANGEL' TV SHOW?

Gramps,
As for me, "Touched by an Angel" is a lovely show. But if you listen carefully, they do suggest that angels are of a different race than humans and will never have the human experience; God is everywhere and nowhere, etc. That doesn't really go along with our beliefs. It is filmed in and around SLC? And I love Della Reese. Does that count?
Brenda

Dear Brenda,
A television show is a television show, produced in Salt Lake City or anywhere else. This is not an LDS production and has no relationship with the church whatsoever. I agree with you that it is one of the less offensive shows in terms of moral values, and it exemplifies faith in God. It is one of the few TV shows that I enjoy watching, but I would never attempt to read any doctrinal issues into the show. We receive eternal truth from the Holy Scriptures and from the words of the prophets.
—Gramps

WHAT DOES THE "F" STAND FOR IN JOSEPH F. SMITH'S NAME?

Gramps,
What does the initial "F" stand for in Joseph F. Smith? And how did he get that name?
John, from Ohio

Dear John,
The "F" in President Smith's name stands for Fielding, which was the maiden name of his mother, Mary Fielding, who was born in England on July 21, 1801. Mary emigrated to Canada where she was converted to the church in Toronto by Parley P. Pratt. She then came to Kirtland, Ohio, where she married Hyrum Smith, the Prophet's brother, on December 24, 1837. Joseph Fielding Smith was born in Far West, Missouri on November 13, 1838.
—Gramps

WHAT WOULD BE THE FUNCTIONS OF BODY ORGANS IN THE RESURRECTION?

Gramps,
This is a comment regarding eating and sleeping in the hereafter. Parley P. Pratt wrote that every organ we have is destined for use in the resurrection. I believe he is quoted in Talmadge's "Articles of Faith" in a chapter endnote.
—Ken from Arizona

Dear Ken,
You are undoubtedly referring to the quotation of Elder Parley P. Pratt in the *Key to the Science of Theology*, Ch. 6 p.53, which says about resurrected man:
> *"Filling the measure of his responsibilities in the world of spirits, he passes by means of the resurrection of the body, into his fourth*

estate, or sphere of human existence. In this sphere he finds himself clothed upon with an eternal body of flesh and bones, with every sense and every organ restored and adapted to their proper use."

Elder Bruce R. McConkie also said:

"These are the words of Amulek. 'Now, there is a death which is called a temporal death,' he continues. 'And the death of Christ shall loose the bands of this temporal death, that all shall be raised from this temporal death. The spirit and the body shall be reunited again in its perfect form.' There will be no physical imperfections in the resurrection, no disease, no corruption, nothing to impair the proper functioning of every organ of the body. 'Both limb and joint shall be restored to its proper frame, even as we now are at this time; and we shall be brought to stand before God, knowing even as we know now and have a bright recollection of all our guilt'." (Bruce R. McConkie, *A New Witness for the Articles of Faith*, p.153)

Elder Pratt says that in the resurrection *"every sense and every organ [will be] restored and adapted to their proper use."* So, here is the question: What will be their proper use in eternity? Very little is said in the scriptures about the organs of the body of a person in eternity, but some things are said. For instance,

Yea, O Lord, how long shall they suffer these wrongs and unlawful oppressions, before thine heart shall be softened toward them, and thy bowels be moved with compassion toward them? (D&C 121:3)

Such statements about the functions of organs could be purely euphemistic, but on the other hand...It would seem rather limiting to suppose that the organs of the body would continue to support mortal functions in a resurrected, eternal being with unlimited capacity.

—Gramps

HOW LONG DID JOSEPH SMITH HAVE THE PLATES OF THE BOOK OF MORMON IN HIS POSSESSION?

Gramps,
How long did Joseph Smith actually have physical possession of the golden plates? Some say three years, and others say ten. Is there historical verification somewhere? Thank you.
—Sheryl, from Utah

Dear Sheryl,
The Prophet received the plates from Moroni in September of 1827, and the translation of the Book of Mormon was completed in June of 1829. After that the plates were returned to the Angel Moroni, who has had them in his custody to this day. However, the date that the plates were returned was not recorded, so those who say three years or ten are only guessing. No one knows.
—Gramps

WHY DOES GOD SEND HANDICAPPED CHILDREN INTO THE WORLD?

Dear Gramps,
We have a daughter who has Down Syndrome. At times she is a joy, but at all times she is a heavy responsibility. Why does God send such children into the world, especially profoundly retarded ones who will never be able to care for themselves?
Ron

Dear Ron,
And as Jesus passed by, he saw a man which was blind from his birth. And his disciples asked him, saying, Master, who did sin, this man, or his parents, that he was born blind? Jesus answered, Neither

hath this man sinned, nor his parents: but that the works of God
should be made manifest in him. (John 9:1-3)

Here is the prime example of why the Lord would bring handi-
capped children into the world. But how are the works of God manifest? Through those who care for these children. One of the noblest
endeavors of man is to care for the less fortunate. The Savior again gave
the example when he told of the good Shepard who left the ninety and
nine and went searching for the one that was lost.

I suppose that we were not unaware, in the pre-mortal spirit world,
of what life would be like in mortality. I can imagine that you had made
a pact with your child who in that state would have volunteered to come
into mortality in a disadvantaged condition to give you the opportunity
to care for her and thus reap the rich blessings promised to those who
sacrifice themselves in compassionate service to others.

Henry Drummond, in his little treatise on love, entitled "The
Greatest Thing In The World," made this cogent statement:

'The greatest thing,' says someone, 'a man can do for his
Heavenly Father is to be kind to some of His other children.' I won-
der why it is that we are not all kinder than we are. How much the
world needs it. How easily it is done. How instantaneously it acts.
How infallibly it is remembered. How superabundantly it pays itself
back–for there is no debtor in the world so honourable, so superbly
honourable, as Love."

It is interesting to consider, in light of your situation, the principles
of priesthood power and influence as found in D&C 121:41-42:

No power or influence can or ought to be maintained by virtue of
the priesthood, only by persuasion, by long-suffering, by gentleness
and meekness, and by love unfeigned; By kindness, and pure knowl-
edge.

Think of these principles of priesthood power and influence– persuasion, long-suffering, gentleness, meekness, love unfeigned and
kindness. They don't just happen to us; they must be acquired and
developed by life's experiences and by how we respond to them.
Someone said, "Authority can never be acquired, it must always be
conferred; while ability can never by conferred, it must always be
acquired."

However, so often when we are faced with unpleasant or difficult circumstances, we ask the question, "Why Me?" The immediate answer is "Why not me?" Rather than asking "Why me?" we should fall on our knees and thank the Lord for the sacred opportunity that He was given us to become more like He is. Here are some of his promises to those who have the strength to be called upon to undergo difficult and trying circumstances during their mortal sojourn:

> *Search diligently, pray always, and be believing, and <u>all things shall work together for your good</u>, if ye walk uprightly and remember the covenant wherewith ye have covenanted one with another.* (D&C 90:24)

> *Verily I say unto you, all among them who know their hearts are honest, and are broken, and their spirits contrite, <u>and are willing to observe their covenants by sacrifice—yea, every sacrifice which I, the Lord, shall command—they are accepted of me</u>. For I, the Lord, will cause them to bring forth as a very fruitful tree which is planted in a goodly land, by a pure stream, that yieldeth much precious fruit.* (D&C 97:8-9)

> *Therefore, he giveth this promise unto you, with an immutable covenant that they shall be fulfilled; and <u>all things wherewith you have been afflicted shall work together for your good</u>, and to my name's glory, saith the Lord.* (D&C 98:3)

> *For after much tribulation, as I have said unto you in a former commandment, cometh the blessing.* (D&C 103:12)

—Gramps

QUESTIONS ABOUT WORLD WAR II

Dear Gramps,
Reading the Infobases Gospel Library about this matter, we would like to ask you the following:
1. Did you see the Larry King show with the Rabbis and the Southern Baptist minister?
2. Did the LDS First Presidency, at the beginning of the 1940s, know that there was a holocaust going on in Germany in WWII?

3. *According to late reports of the American Red Cross, the First Presidency knew.*
4. *Why did they not protest to the government?*
Shalom,
A Reader from Holland

Dear Reader,
1. No.
2. I was in the military forces during the WWII. Near the beginning of the war, we heard rumors that the Jews were being horribly mistreated. As more and more information leaked out, it was absolutely incredulous. It was hard to disbelieve the reports as the atrocities that were reported seemed to be beyond the capability of human depravity! As more evidence was revealed, all doubts were erased, and the American people were horrified!
3. OK, so?
4. Your question presupposes some evil intent on the part of the First Presidency. I cannot imagine such a question being asked unless from it were a direct and rather juvenile attempt to discredit the First Presidency in some way. It is not worthy of an answer.
   —Gramps

HOW CAN I KEEP MY NEW CONVERT FRIEND FROM FALLING BACK INTO HER OLD WAYS?

Dear Gramps,
A dear friend of mine was baptized two years ago into the church. She was a "Golden Convert" and loved everything she learned. Later she moved to a small community with few people her age. She has fallen back into her "old ways" and does not attend church. She wants to come back to church so bad, but feels awful for what she has done. She is also scared to be alone (breaking up with her boyfriend). I pray for her all of the time and she has made several attempts but always falls

into the same trap after only a little while. Do you have any advice other than to pray for her?
   Angela, from Italy

Dear Angela,
   It is very difficult for a new convert to maintain her integrity with regard to the baptismal commitment when she is isolated from the church. However, in her new community there are apparently a few members her age. Often, however, where the branch is small, they may not have the resources to provide the full fellowship that she needs. In fact, they may not even know that she lives there.
   Of prime importance is that you maintain your contact with her. In addition to praying for her, you may want to write her frequent letters. If she has not moved too far away, an occasional visit might do wonders–or you could invite her to visit you over a weekend so that she can attend church with you.
   It may also help if you were to write a letter to the president of the mission that has jurisdiction in that area and suggest that the missionaries visit her from time to time. Hopefully, she will receive strength from you, the missionaries, and her Branch, and be able to resist falling back into her "old ways."
   —Gramps

HOW CAN I HELP MY FAMILY TO BECOME MORE ACTIVE IN THE CHURCH?

Dear Gramps,
My family's sorta inactive. How can I help them?
Julie

Dear Julie,
   When you speak of your family I assume that you're talking about your parents and perhaps other family members. Let's assume for the moment that you're talking about your parents. Regardless of the

reasons for their inactivity, it is almost always counter-productive to try to tell your parents what you think that they should do. It is not normal for parents to take instruction from their children. In the case of children's taking advise and being obedient to parents, however, the roles are reversed.

There is something you can do that could have a powerful effect for good on your parents. If you, alone, were to attend church faithfully and live strictly in accordance with the doctrines and teachings of the church, your parents would see how living the principles of the gospel is a source of happiness, promotes moral principles, and enjoins respect from children for parents. When they see the beneficial effects of the gospel in your life–how much the church means to you and the joy and happiness and fulfilment that it brings to you—they may begin to realize that they could receive the same benefits through their own acceptance of gospel principles and participation in church activities.

If you show your parents by your actions that you love them, that you honor and respect them, and that you are obedient to their instructions, you will preach a sermon to them much more powerful than any that could be put in words.

—Gramps

How can I help a young man in our Ward become more active?

Dear Gramps,

A young man in my ward, who is my age, comes to church only because his parents make him. He passes the sacrament, but does not attend Sunday School. He is nice person, but is not living up to what the prophets and scriptures have told him to do. Our youth have been trying to get him to come to activities, but the only other reason he comes to church, other than Sunday Sacrament meetings, is if he can use the gym for basketball. We want him to come, but each week he seems to slip farther away from the gospel. We pray for him, but nothing seems to be working. What should the youth do when his parents don't care enough to help?

Sarah, from Washington State

Dear Sarah,

As you well know, the teenage years are difficult times, and especially so in the world of today. Each young person must make up his or her mind as to what direction to take in life. But there is nothing like genuine love, respect, and friendship to help a person feel wanted and desire to change.

You already may be doing these things, but perhaps the young man in your ward could best be helped if the sincerity of the friendship for him went beyond attempts to get him out to church. If he were included in some of your family activities or other group activities, he might begin to feel more a part of the group. Your praying for him is very important. It is also extremely important to never give up.

—Gramps

ARE ALL CALLINGS TO SERVE MADE BY INSPIRATION?

Dear Gramps,

I am struggling with the concept that all leaders are called by inspiration. I have had experiences where I have witnessed questionable behavior by my bishops and stake presidents. I have heard incredibly insensitive statements and viewed unseemly actions by leaders. My question is, how can this be if calls are inspired? Surely the Lord knows that the man is dishonest! Therefore, I have concluded that the person's outward service was the main influence in his call.

Anonymous

Dear Anonymous,

Apparently you are of the opinion that the Lord only calls church leaders who have no faults. If that were the case, the church would be without leadership, for there are no people without faults. *If we say that we have no sin, we deceive ourselves, and the truth is not in us.* (1 John 1:8) My impression is that the Lord calls people to service in His kingdom for two reasons: 1) to bless the lives of those whom they have the honor to serve, and 2) to learn and grow in the gospel from the opportunity of serving others. I would imagine that at least fifty-one percent of the reason for church callings is the latter. We grow from serving, not from being served. Brigham Young said,

> *"With all the rest of the good that you can commit to memory, be sure to recollect that the Gospel of salvation is expressly designed to make Saints of sinners, to overcome evil with good, to make holy, good men of wicked, bad men, and to make better men of good."* (Discourses of Brigham Young, p.448 - p.449)

If we are consumed with criticism for the faults of others we make ourselves bitter and unhappy. Often those of whom we are critical have no idea of our attitude, so the only person we hurt is ourselves. When I was in basic training in Shepard Field, Texas in 1942, I went to church in a little branch in Wichita Falls. On one occasion I attended sort of a conference, and Elder Harold B. Lee, of the Council of the Twelve was the speaker. During his talk he made a simple statement that touched my heart in such a way that I have never forgotten. He simply said, "Be kind, forgiving, and overlook the faults of others."

The burden of a bishop is a heavy one. He needs all the support that he can get. We needn't demand that he be without fault, or that all his judgments and decisions be impeccable. Let him pursue his administration according to the dictates of his own conscience. If we have raised our hands to sustain him as bishop, we are obligated to the Lord to do all we can to aid, support, assist, and help him to succeed in his calling. We don't need to agree with his decisions or his direction, but discretion would dictate that we keep such differences to ourselves to ensure that we don't promote disunity in the ward. Then, if we are faithful and serve where we can with diligence, the Lord may then call us, with all our faults, to be the bishop.

—Gramps

WHERE DID THE TERM "JACK MORMON" COME FROM?

Dear Gramps,
My question is, where did the term "Jack Mormon" come from?
—Oryanstar, from Arizona

Dear Oryanstar,
It seems that the term "Jack Mormon" was coined by a man named Sharp, who was an anti-Masonic editor in western New York State. He invented the name "Jack Mason" for all persons who refused to take part in the anti-Masonic movement of that time and place. Sharp was also anti-Mormon and coined the name "Jack Mormon" for all those who were not Mormons but who did not favor the illegal procedure and mob violence of Sharp and his associates against the Mormons.

Today the term is frequently used for those who are members of the LDS Church, but who are inactive.
—Gramps

AS A DIVORCED, LARGER FEMALE, HOW CAN I FIND A MAN WHO IS NOT BOTHERED BY SIZE?

Dear Gramps,
Do you have any suggestions on how to met older singles. I have been a member of the church for 22 years and I am now a 46 year old female. It is very hard to find a good single Mormon man to date. I am also a larger woman and so it's even harder to find a man that size does not bother. I have been single the whole time I've been in the church. I was divorced prior to joining the church. It would be nice to just go on a date and feel like a woman again. Sincerely,
Susan, from Cleveland, Ohio

Dear Susan,

I can imagine how lonely it feels not to be included in the dating activities of others with whom you associate. You mention that you are a larger woman, and you're right that it's hard to find a man that size does not bother. There is no doubt that if men knew of the wonderful qualities of your character and personality, there would be many who would not be bothered because you are a larger woman. Look at all the people who are both obese and happily married.

The significant truth is that practically none of them were overweight until after they learned to love one another. Unfortunately, men are almost universally attracted first by appearance and then by personality and then by intellect and then by character–the exact opposite of the value that they attach to each of those four personal qualities. So it looks like if you want to have a social life you have a price to pay. You must be willing to make the sacrifice to lose all your excess weight or you will by default sacrifice your social life. The definition of sacrifice is to give up something of value for something else of greater value.

I recognize that losing weight is no easy thing, especially if the weight problem is long term. But there is no question but that it can be done, and is being done by many people. So, as you come to terms with the issues that are at stake, you will take that course of action that is most meaningful to you.

—Gramps